Sue Johnston is an 83-year old widow who loves travelling and driving her Honda Jazz car about the country. She also enjoys walking across fields and woods, exploring the scenery. She familiarises herself with modern technological devices to help her have a leisurely tour. Sue only drives 80–100 miles a day, parking at the next hotel, then investigating the local sights on foot. She usually only spends two half-days at each destination, having reserved the very efficient booking.com for bedtime.

To my late husband, Ray; also to my family, who say he would be very proud of me.

Sue Johnston

GRAN TOUR OF THE UK

AUSTIN MACAULEY PUBLISHERS™

LONDON • CAMBRIDGE • NEW YORK • SHARJAH

A CIP catalogue record for this title is available from the British Library.

ISBN 9781528900799 (Paperback)
ISBN 9781528957229 (ePub e-book)

www.austinmacauley.com

First Published (2019)
Austin Macauley Publishers Ltd
25 Canada Square
Canary Wharf
London
E14 5LQ

To my publishers, to Booking.com, TomTom, iPad, iPhone and Honda, who all contributed in making my tour possible, leisurely and enjoyable.

I am an eighty-two-year-old widow seeking adventure before hanging up my travelling bag. The angle is of an ancient person using modern technology. A four-year-old *Honda Jazz* is the transport. The Tour takes me round the UK from my home in Sussex, in an anti-clockwise direction, going to Brighton, Hastings and Ramsgate at the start. I'm heading as far North as Strathpeffer beyond Inverness in Scotland, driving eighty to hundred miles a day. This allows plenty of exploring time. I am going by myself.

The challenge is in using modern aids, such as satnav (TomTom), *iPad* and *iPhone* to help with plans. I am spending time experimenting and trying out these 'complicated' devices, relying on the younger members of my family to guide me.

My car is my wardrobe, office, snack bar and navigation hub. I leave everything in the car overnight while at my bnb, except the devices, my toilet bag and tomorrow's clothes. I use Airbnb and Booking.com to find all accommodation along the twenty-five hundred miles, thirty-two different places. Arriving at my destination, parking at the bnb, setting out to investigate the area, I walk about four to five miles each day. I decide where I might eat in the evening. Sometimes my hotel is good. Sometimes I find a different restaurant or pub in the venue. I enjoy the solitary style of observing my fellows as I go.

My leisurely pace is quite relaxing, not being fazed either by busy motorways or long, lonely country lanes in the highlands. I study the local brochure at each hotel for tips about today's visit. I discover all about the Devil's Porridge Museum near Gretna this way, the most interesting bit of history.

I endeavour to pass on tips using my devices, for other intrepid travellers, (I used to teach word processing in the old days!) this may be a geographical lesson in covering the country in a fun way! Everything has gone according to plan. There are no horror stories, just an interesting adventure with a happy ending. Now I plan the next Tour.

Marvellous, reliable, smart, efficient, capacious, economical, an all-round good egg: my dark blue *Honda Jazz* car came to me three years old, having only done nineteen thousand miles, in May 2016. I have had six months of minor journeys, getting to do neat parking in reverse in very narrow car parks, as a challenge. I have even transported my Christmas tree by folding down the back passenger seat, as well as taking three large bags of garden rubbish to the tip by putting the back seats down.

Being an eighty-two-year-old widow for a year, means I am getting used to being independent after sixty years of marriage (teamwork!). January 2017 came and went. It was only in March I have to renew my driving licence; 'No MOT' says the online form. Rang the garage where I bought it. "We've stopped doing *Honda* now," they told me. No notification to me about my MOT Test. "No problem. We can do it next week," says my very helpful local Pat's Garage.

"I could have been fined over the past three months I've been without it," I commented to them.

Now my challenge begins – *Google* gives me a Video of 'Pre-MOT Test Check'.

"It only takes two minutes." OK, Checking the seat belts involves lots of crawling about in the back especially as there are three there! Then the front ones. Find the levers to change the seat heights etc. and then the bonnet release – easy as it is to the right of the steering wheel, with a picture of bonnet on it!

I've done this before. I know I have to put my hand under top of bonnet and feel for a lever to push sideways. (Oh, it might be oily, so I have a garage rag to hand). Success! Prop up bonnet lid with rod provided. Now to find the windscreen washer stick. Apparently one and a half million people's cars fail the test as their washer water is too low.

What a long, curly stick it is! I wipe it and gradually feed it back in and out again. "Goodness me, less than half an inch of water in there; don't panic." It may be Bank Holiday Monday, but *Google* will tell me where I can get supplies. Put rod back, slam (Sorry Honda) bonnet shut, collect purse. "Do you need concentrated or diluted?" A handsome young assistant comes armed with a funnel to do the job for me.

"I've not done this before. I don't drive yet," he explains. I've chosen diluted. Back home to continue checks: oil, OK, then tyres – use a 20p piece to insert in groove of each tyre to see if it is fine. All three pass, but the offside front (I'm getting technical now!) is slightly lower. This all took me more than two minutes!

Tomorrow comes. "Can I watch you?" I even go under the ramp (how brave) and see the brakes etc. "I had no idea the Test is so comprehensive," I remark to Tony.

"You will need a replacement tyre when you have your interim service," he says.

"To match the others?" I comment knowingly!

"I know how they choose a replacement cricket ball when one is lost or damaged during a match. The twelfth man brings out a boxful of slightly used ones onto the pitch, the two umpires then choose one with the right number of overs' use."

"Just like that," he says.

After *Jazz*'s interim service and new tyre, total cost £263, I resolve to DO SOMETHING interesting in my newly spruced up *Honda*. I like driving so decide to do a GRAN Tour of the UK

The family is all in favour. I arrange extra car insurance, buy the extras needed. Then importantly, I plan the arrangement of accoutrements in my car, a special map to position all my possessions for a two-month adventure. I'm ready to go.

Chapter 1
The Plans

"I'm planning to go round the UK in my car," was my pronouncement to the family three months ago.

"Yes, by myself to have an adventure."

"Oh, OK," they said.

So I did. I spent six weeks in the planning. The two pilot sessions I arranged (wisely it turned out) were my very first trial with my TOMTOM sat nav. I also had my *iPhone* and my *iPad* as my foray into modern technology!

I have a *Honda Jazz* car that is four years old and quite nippy I think! (I mean my car!) It had an interim service and one new tyre – "specially chosen to match the wear on the other three," I was informed by my expert garage man. There you are – I'm all set to go!

Must do it now before I get any older and greyer and less fit – I am eighty-two after all. I've been a widow for fifteen months now. I must DO something, especially as my car is raring to go. That's a point, must ring the car insurance people to see if they need to know. I usually say my limit is three thousand miles per year. I think it will be quite a few more on this occasion.

My first trial is to Brighton, a chance to try out my TomTom, a day out with a visit to the RNLI lifeboat station to see if I could incorporate some fundraising for them. Leave home at 6:30 a.m. – well, you know what Brighton is like in mid-summer, don't you? Even if you don't live there, the same photos are produced on the beach of people packed like sardines on the seashore... Anyway arrive by successful satnav at the multi storey car park in the Marina at 7:30 a.m. Only two other cars there! Plenty of room for *Jazz*.

My first victory – obeying the sat nav, come what may!

No one at the Lifeboat Station – oh oh, they're only there when there's an emergency at sea! Silly me. The guys in the Marina office take pity on me and invite me into their office for a cup of coffee. They tell me the plans for the moving of the lifeboat station soon. The supporting gift shop only opens when volunteers arrive later in the morning.

News about the Brighton lifeboat – it is being floated from its present mooring to a more convenient place at the other side of the harbour as soon as the piles are in place. I won't be there to see it. If I'd like a photo with the whole crew, just come down on training evening (Tuesday) or Sunday when the station is open for viewing. Sorry, I should be on my Tour by then. My first 'Event Missed'. There are many others. I'm not in a hurry, but there is only one weekend per week to have Open Days, Fetes and Beer Fests. What a shame!

Off to find somewhere for breakfast – wander about till 9:00 a.m. My very first Tour meal! The pattern of days to come. By the end I will have denuded the country of scrambled eggs and mushrooms! That, with brown toast and a big mug of real coffee and I'm set up for whatever lies ahead! At my advanced years, I have to steer clear of anything pertaining to the PIG – hence my eschewment of bacon and sausage! So sad when I see plates of full English piling up around me as I sit in solitary state with my aforementioned repast!

Full up and ready to go home, I retrace my steps to the multi-storey car park. Oh dear! My car has gone! "*Jazz*, where are you?" At least the space is there! Having arrived as only the third car in the whole place, now it is full to bursting, "Where is my jalopy?" Don't panic! Is this the end of my Tour before it has even begun?

No one to ask. "Be calm. It must be here."

Make a systematic search of floor 2. Phew! There it is – diagonally opposite where I'd imagined it to be. A car park syndrome I believe! Sit for a few minutes to calm down.

"Now TomTom do your stuff – you know my home post code, get to it." I've got the volume right up high, so when he addresses me I jump out of my skin! He is quiet for so long when I'm not expected to turn off any particular road! Still this Trial Run is just for such things to be assessed.

We get home. TomTom is Australian by the way. He has a wicked sense of humour. I keep him as my voice of choice as my late husband set him up when we got him. (TomTom, not my husband!)

Now, Tomtom's final remark after every successful journey is: "You have reached your destination. Windows up, put on your sunnies and don't let the seagulls steal your chips." After thirty-six days on the road, I find this strangely comforting, even though we had a lot of rain!

Sixty miles driving today, walking for about three, friends with TomTom and ready for the next Trial, must find TT's volume control before we set off again. Must load the app for 'find my car' – another marvellous invention my grandson told me about. I am determined to come to grips with this modern technology: TomTom (sat nav), *iPhone* and *iPad*.

As well as all my old-fashioned pages and pages of hand-written notes, post-its, map books and journals – no, I will not be caught out! I've now spent five weeks in the planning! Even got as far as making a detailed layout for my *Jazz* on its travels. Not to mention Dartmouth and Cuthbert who will be accompanying me…

Look out for Trial Number Two where I spend the night in a stranger's house. How I'm learning the ins and outs of my devices, the charging thereof, the storing of them overnight, what to take into the Bnb so I don't give the impression I have come for a fortnight, and above all. "Have I parked the car in an approved spot for this evening?" And "Oh, what is your Wi-Fi code and password please?"

Chapter 2
Trial Night at Bnb – Hastings

Off with *Jazz* and TomTom to Hastings for my first night alone at a bnb. I was vetted and registered with Air-bnb when I booked in, of course. "Will there be a lock on my door? Will my host be pleased to see me? Can I manage up two flights of stairs with my heavy bags?" Solutions to be revealed. Stop at Battle for a coffee and to try out my find-my-car app. TomTom has brought me to Hastings very well.

Trouble begins when we have to find the lifeboat station and parking! This adds a few miles to my driving this morning. Haven't factored in the cost of car parking into my budget! £4.30 for the day there, a long tricky walk along the beach to find the RNLI, took several good pictures of the lifeboat on my *iPhone*. The gift shop is very well stocked. The ladies there floor my ambitions to raise funds for the lifeboats. "You're not getting sponsorship? No one will just give you money… You're not jogging, hopping, cycling or walking." Oh dear – collapse of stout party!

My plan is to drive eighty to hundred miles a day, park *Jazz* at the bnb and then go on walk – about to explore the area, hopefully as much along the coast as possible, chatting to lifeboat folk. I just realised there are none of the crews at the stations unless it's Open Day or they have a call-out. Never mind, there will always be lifeguards to interview.

Tramp along the cobbled beach then sit and eat my picnic lunch. Sunny day. I'd forgotten the pesky seagulls! They keep swooping down on me silently. I arm myself with a few beach pebbles just to deter them you understand – eating a gooey bun full of egg mayo and looking up constantly to view the opposition doesn't make for good digestion!

The next 'fun watch' is a family who set out their rugs and picnics near the sea. They don't know the tide is coming in. Halfway through their meal, a gentle little wave creeps up and all over everything! Mum quickly flings the shoes and spare clothes up behind her. The children shriek, "Oh Granddad, your trousers are all wet."

"My sandals are floating."

Doesn't anyone make visitors to beaches aware that the tide comes in and out? As a solitary person, I find observing people very amusing. They don't notice me as they are occupied with their own activities.

Enjoy my sunny afternoon on the beach – find it difficult to get up on the moving pebbles! As a treat, I queue to buy a ninety-nine ice cream. I start to eat it and the cone collapses!

Oops, all down my arm and blouse. Totter back to stall "Er, could you help me please" and the kind lady offers me a bowl and spoon to decant it. Search for extra tissues in my pockets. Note to self: Make sure I always have many tissues in all pockets for just such eventualities.

TomTom then programmed to my first bnb. He sits proudly on *Jazz*'s dashboard on a special suction pad. Having made a specific note of all the postcodes for every hotel or guesthouse, it should be easy to find my first room for the night. I have to follow TT implicitly. He takes me along some back lanes and roads which only he knows about!

I can't use his map on the screen as the light on the dashboard where he sits is too glaring. Therefore I just have his lovely Australian voice to follow to the ends of the UK – nearly! Being of the old school, I do still plot the route on my real (hard copy?) map. It's an Aldi one, so useful if I need supplies wherever I am.

Back to Hastings. The guesthouse is in St Leonard's on Sea. I type in the postcode, press 'done', position TT on the dashboard and set off.

"Turn right after three hundred yards," he says. I'm still trying to work out what three hundred yards looks like. I always remember the hundred yards marked at school on the field for Sports Day. I never liked it. I was useless at running! Don't turn right straight away. He said, "Three hundred yards."

"Oh bother," I turned too soon. I'm in the bus station.

Arrive at the correct road, "You have reached your destination, windows up, put on your sunnies and don't let the seagulls steal your chips!" advises TT. I found the address, collected one small suitcase, having prepared it with one night's gear, and carry it with difficulty up the twelve steps to the house. Everything in St Leonard's residential area is on a steep hill it seems.

Welcomed by my first host and given a coffee in their sitting room and shown up more stairs to my room, very pleasant with view of their very steep garden, sunny still, after spreading out my belongings on chair and floor (more details later), I walk about 1.5 miles downhill to the seaside to find supper. Making a note of way home, it won't be dark by nine p.m.-ish, one reason for doing my Tour in summer.

Have yummy pizza and a glass of red wine on the seafront. I must get over the shy feeling of asking for a table for one now. Enjoy watching my fellow diners and the food they choose. "Large people order large pizzas," I'd say. Sea is very calm; walk along the front a while. Then tackle the steep walk home. I have remembered to bring my door's keys and cleverly, I thought, I had tried out my front door key in the lock as I left for supper, to make sure it fits.

The Wi-Fi and passcode are found on a tiny piece of paper in a drawer in my room. Set them up in my iPhone and iPad ready to do something (?) later. That is, I go into settings, type in Wi-Fi name, unless it comes up automatically on the screen, and then very carefully type in the passcode. If it doesn't like it, try again. If it still won't play ball, go downstairs and ask for help! "It won't always work in your room," they say helpfully! Next exercise is fitting devices on charge overnight. I have a double USB socket which will take both the iPad and iPhone plugged in. Then the wall socket switched on. I must make sure they are fully at 100% each morning.

As for TomTom, he is a different matter. He has his own socket and cable. He will be plugged in to the wall, switched on for an hour before I go to bed each night. He just needs a boost I think, as he is automatically charged in the car as I go along. A special USB socket in the car is where his long cable is attached.

He sits on the dashboard after I have given him the latest postcode, press 'done', and we're off to our next destination. If I leave him switched on in the bedroom overnight, he has been known to say something like: "Turn round when possible," which is a bit concerning in the middle of the night!

Maybe there can be an electricity glitch. So he sleeps when I do. I have a special zippy-up bag where I neatly stow my devices' cables and plugs, to ensure I don't leave them behind each morning before starting next journey. Put tomorrow's top and panties ready. I am not having a shower as their bath has not a handle for me to climb in and out…

Chapter 3
Bexhill in the Sunshine!

I get up early as I think of so much to do. Make a cuppa very careully in my room. Did I mention I have stiff fingers and wrists which makes simple tasks a bit hazardous at times! I haven't arranged breakfast here. I don't want to wait till after 9 a.m. to get going, so I decide to pack up and leave. There is no one around, so I write a little 'thank you' note, leaving the keys too, and creep down the two flights of stairs with my bags. I'm not sure of the form really, this being my very first bnb!

I have the whole day in front of me so decide on Bexhill the nearest seaside. Program TomTom to take me to the Beach café. I don't know if there is one, but TomTom needs a goal (address) and agrees to my suggestion. By now it is 8:45 a.m. – no sign of tourists along the front at Bexhill.

I find the café called Sovereign Light Café after the lighthouse far off the shore from here. I park *Jazz* easily near the café for breakfast when I've had my walk. Set up my 'find car' app as directed by Lewis (Grandson). Press the app, follow instructions to orientate the compass and the screen says, "You parked here." Five yards away. So that seems OK. It'll be a good test when I come back, even though I can see *Jazz* now!

A few dog walkers along the prom on a very sunny, calm morning. Dogs' leads get longer and longer; beware tripping over them if you should stop to take in the sights! Sometimes on a later trip in a crowded tourist street, you can mistake what is on the end of the lead – not necessarily a dog that looks like its owner, but a toddler that is the image of his dad!

One mile is enough for an appetite, so return to café (*Jazz* is still there; says 'find' app). Lovely big plate of scrambled eggs and mushrooms on toast – must ask for smaller portion in future. Big mug of coffee to go with it. Walking further along to find the loo, I come across a beautiful seaside garden with things for kids to do. Over at the edge of the sea, the Surf Rescue Camp has set up its banner.

All ages of youngsters are donning wet suits and preparing for a day of surf training. They have obviously chosen this week as the tide is very low, which means they will have plenty of waist-high water to practise in.

Collect my beach towel and yesterday's flask of coffee from *Jazz*'s boot and choose a spot near the breakwater, which I could lean on and watch the surfers too. Have a paddle! Tricky on this pebbly beach, but some sand has appeared so that is just right. "Oh dear, I can't balance on one leg to dry my foot and put my sandal on." Thinks: 'Could sit on pebbles, but how to get up again is the question.' Must think of going back to Tai Chi next winter to remedy that and improve my balance.

Group of six young people arrive complete with enormous cool box, rugs and towels. Whole beach to choose from, where did they sit? Five metres away from me! Still, amusing, as I can watch them and be unnoticed. A single person is no threat to anyone and goes completely unseen when there are two or more people together. I love people-watching.

I notice the numbered breakwaters for people doing healthy walking. A few joggers were emerging as were cyclists who were weaving among strollers on the prom. Walk over to the Bexhill Pavilion, a very smart building, recently renovated, with art galleries, shops, café and an auditorium. Outside is an amusing water feature of moving fountains which children eagerly run in and out of, in the warm sunshine. Parents sit at the edge holding their spare clothes.

Back to the café for my salad. Tested *Jazz* app again and left for home, putting my postcode into TomTom. Well, this is a test run, so I must do things properly! I stopped at Uckfield for a kilo of cherries. Disaster! As I pull in to the lay-by, TomTom falls (or jumps?) off the dashboard and switches off! No sign of my destination on his screen, nothing. Sat for a minute contemplating – is it low battery? Have I broken him? Never mind. I do know my way home from here anyway! Sort him out later. Yummy cherries anyhow.

Home at 5 p.m. Lots of notes about my second trial. I make several more bookings for my tour starting in two weeks' time.

Make a map of the inside of my *Honda Jazz*. Try out my two small suitcases to fit on the back seat. Shoes to go in the well behind the driver's seat, my hessian bag I will call my 'office' will go on the floor of the front passenger's side, containing all my paperwork, maps and booking details ready to hand. I have my main map on the passenger seat, in case of diversions or my change of mind as I journey along! Dartmouth and Cuthbert are my passengers.

In the boot, I have a cool bag to put fruit and drinks in. Also my special clothes bag holds my towelling robe, dressing gown and slippers and tomorrow's panties and clean blouse and trousers.

My tiny cool bag is for my medication. It goes back right of the boot, covered by a spare towel (feet for the drying of). It contains a freezer bag that I occasionally ask my host to put in her freezer overnight. It will keep everything cold for the journey. Also: a fold-up chair, a rucksack and some light walking boots put in the bottom of the boot. That is where I have small tools, a triangle, a jack and a hi-viz jacket. Still some space for anything else I might need. "Oh, by the way I have a corner for any small souvenirs or presents I may buy."

Describe my 'passengers': Dartmouth and Cuthbert. Dartmouth is my teddy bear (Guess where he came from?) and his new friend Cuthbert was given me as a mascot – he's bright green and may have come from Loch Ness. I'll have to see when I get there. Anyhow, they will sit in the passenger seat with seat belt and act as my safety net! "Sorry, I can't stop. Dartmouth is waiting for me…" So it is not obvious that I am alone, should I be propositioned. (I am dreaming!)

Chapter 4
Ramsgate

Planning is still going apace. My friend comes to enquire progress, "And where after Kinross?" she asks. More lists come out."

"Booking of Dartford Tunnel and payment in advance, or you may get fined if you leave it too late," I tell her.

"Where to hide house keys? Shall I switch water off? What about post, especially junk mail that gets stuffed in the letter box?" She's tired at the thoughts!

"Family lives nearby and will be popping in from time to time," I explain.

The start is here. *Jazz* loaded, TomTom loaded, papers cancelled, gardening arranged and housework on hold… Off we go, off to the first night at Ramsgate. Raining as I leave, typical as we've just had a heat wave of eighty degrees till now. TomTom doesn't tell me where he's going – at least I haven't yet learnt how to ask him – so I just drive exactly where he says – Motorway to start with. That's OK for me as I always seemed to get the wet driving sections when my late husband and I shared all the driving. Several downpours greet me, lorries throwing up sheets of water, wipers going full pelt and then a twenty-minute stop in a traffic jam.

Here I learn how to pull into the side to let an ambulance go by. Stop at Detling Bangers Café for three American pancakes and maple syrup for my breakfast. What is this? I've never had such a dish before. I must be branching out in my old age. I even ask for an extra jug of syrup! I have to ask the waiter, "Where am I?" TomTom hadn't mentioned my stop. I contacted my son-in-law to ask him, "If TomTom carries on where we left off in the car park?"

Good. Got an instant answer, "yes, he does." That's reassuring and another fact learnt! Get to Ramsgate seafront and manage to park snugly at the side of the road free! I did a lot of practice parking at home – seeing a space at the side of the road, driving up parallel to the car in front then reverse and left-hand down to take up only space left along the road. Pleased with myself. Put on my Car-Finder before I leave the *Jazz*, who knows where I am going on foot now! The other main car park, under the very high cliffs, that I surveyed is £4 per hour.

Go down on the lift to the harbour, round the Maritime Museum. Meet a very interesting couple who have just sailed over from Dunkirk in their Legend thirty-three feet sailing boat called Summer Wine. "They are an older couple that were widowed and just palled up for sailing," the lady explains.

They have just done eleven hours sailing over from Belgium. Tell me the Belgians wanted to charge them a fine for using red diesel which is all you can get in UK. The fines can be £500 if they find evidence, when they dip into your tank. They risk leaving anyway and get back safely to Ramsgate. The Maritime Museum is an interesting building which houses the RNLI lifeboat station as well as many seafaring artefacts to be studied. It was built as The Clock House in 1817 is now Grade 11 listed and had its second floor designed by John Rennie. It has "a stone-domed clock room in central tower".

The whole is very impressive as it seems to dominate the harbour. Only £2.50 to go in, with informative panels of life at sea! Currently there is a Dunkirk film showing. Ramsgate was the principal place the boats operated from in World War Two. This is the venue for lots of activities around the town. I shall miss the costumed walks scheduled for tonight as I have lots of booking to attend to. When the time comes anyway – it is raining!

Go along the front, into the Queen's Head for coffee and watch some tennis on a giant screen near the bar. Konta wins. Then back up the cliff lift, testing my Find-Car app and there is *Jazz*! "I parked here," says my *iPhone* screen. Off to Arklow Square, Ramsgate my bed for the night, via TomTom of course.

Host's son Neil meets me, shows me round and makes me coffee. Two bathrooms, one with shower, small single room with leafy view of the garden, house on four floors into basement. Very noisy seagulls all around. Didn't see Karen (my host). Ask Neil to put my fridge bag in freezer for me overnight. *Jazz* is very hot at moment. Must remember to ask for bag in the morning.

Off with my *iPhone* map to seafront for yummy crab salad and glass of red wine (not driving till tomorrow). Succumbed to 'Chocolatey Heaven' for pud – a bit gooey, but then I only had pancakes for a late breakfast, didn't I! Back up the hill, all quiet – have my own key for front door and room. Sort out clothes and plugs.

Oops, only 4% left on my *iPhone*, *iPad*, OK. TT needed charging later just before bed! Did my journal the old-fashioned way – exercise book and biro! Also my accounts. Breakfast is not included here.

Amir Rasavi from the Brighton Argus rang me unexpectedly on my *iPhone* this morning with lots of questions about my Tour. I was a bit miffed as I'd already sent him a detailed email on my *iPad* with all plans. People generally don't give their emails more than a cursory glance then forget them I suspect! Still I must respect modern technology, mustn't I? Can't see if anything was published, as my local paper is the East Grinstead Courier where my new friend Sam Truelove gives me an accurate write-up of my Tour. Friends are keeping the cutting for me as I've gone already!

Chapter 5
Chelmsford

Wed, 12th:

Have a coffee in their chaotic kitchen/dining room. Son and daughter at home. Meet Karen my host as I am trying to leave; can't open the front door! Leave at 9:20 a.m. *Jazz* is quite happy at the side of the road near the house in this residential street. TomTom tricky around Ramsgate as I did one roundabout twice! On to Dartford crossing. Pretty scenery on the way, quite flat. Have breakfast; coffee and panini at a tiny, one-horse place! I concentrate well for the M2 and on to Dartford crossing.

TomTom gives precise instructions. Route to Chelmsford going OK. I see a wooded, pretty green park and decide to stop for a break to eat my scratch lunch (left-overs from the fridge and some fruit) at Galleywood, just on the outskirts of Chelmsford. Watch a man let out a big basket of pigeons. They circle once and then fly off. Have a stroll in the sunshine. I set my TT to 'High Street Chelmsford' and hope to find parking when I get there, as I haven't got a postcode for any particular place in town. Don't know how to ask TT for tips yet!

Very difficult locating the entrance to the car park! In fact, once I heard shouting and waving of arms by concerned pedestrians – "Oh, what now?" I realise I am slowly driving along a pedestrianised road – I was slightly exasperated as I had driven round the town several times to find the entrance to the car park!

Eventually I find my way up to the top floor of the multi-storey, thankfully parking *Jazz* for a while. As I leave, I remember to program my *iPhone* for returning to the car. Picturesque corner of this town with the River Chelmer running through it. I enjoy a stroll up and down both sides of the riverbank, on this lovely warm, sunny afternoon. Grassy banks and a parade of thirteen ducks patrolling the edges. Two haughty swans look on.

Three fluffy baby ducklings seem as if they are flying as they skim like balls of fluff along the water behind their mother. Back to *Jazz*. Disaster – TomTom wouldn't work! Luckily, there is a car-wash man nearby. He climbs in the driving seat and inspects my connections, re-arranges them and TT started again! I have a lot to learn. Arrive at Langdale Gardens, Chelmsford, a pretty cul-de-sac where I am staying the night. Helene my host makes me a cuppa and then proceeds to give her pupil a French lesson as I sit in the conservatory.

I arrive a bit early, she expected me about 7 p.m. she said, but is quite happy for me to wait for the room. I must get into the habit of checking my hosts' latest instructions on my *iPhone* before arriving. It was a real French lesson I hasten to add! While waiting for my room, I investigate the way to town for supper on my map and my *iPhone*. I'm not yet very good with the latter.

As I go out for supper I follow *iPhone* implicitly and it takes me exactly the wrong way to town. I walk for an hour as I hadn't realised the minutes to town were going up not down on the screen. The little shop where I bought a Solero has no idea where my bnb is. I retrace my steps and find a Lidl store which is just closing. Rush in and grab two little meat pies and a yoghurt for my supper.

Return to base along a very busy main road. (The town is the other way!) Not a very good start to an extensive Tour of the UK you may say. Eat my meagre repast and a pear and coke in my room. Have a refreshing shower, using my own towelling robe which is my treat. Drying myself with my hands is rather tricky these days. So I keep my robe in its own bag in the car boot. I drape it in there if it's damp after its night on duty! Must now plan tomorrow at Maldon. Have a late breakfast in the kitchen as my host is busy. *Jazz* is ready. Directed TT to take me from this handy cul-de-sac to Maldon sail loft on the front.

Maldon:

TT fell off the dashboard, but still chatted away with full instructions! Must check how to fit him securely on his pad. Remember to set Car Finder at main car park, parking *Jazz* for the whole day safely for £4. Off to explore St Mary's Church on the hill to the beach. A Norman Church with one tiny window preserved from those days, the rest Victorian.

They are having trouble with the walls as the Victorians used the wrong plaster when they renovated the church. Now it all has to be painstakingly scraped off, left for several months to dry and replaced with plaster that breathes! There are some sweet, picturesque cottages on the steep hill down to the water.

At last, a view of the lovely Thames Sailing Barges that I have come to see. They are up to eighty-five feet long and have spectacular dark red sails. All are preserved and rescued from various places. Trips can be taken when the tide is right. They can be hired and entered in barge matches in the sailing season. Two well-known ones are Pudge and Centaur. In the sunshine, I walk along the very well-maintained prom, past the inner lake surrounded with lovely pink flowers, rose-bay-willow herb, purple loosestrife and reeds.

Along to see several cafés with outside seating, another park area and a historical Museum which unfortunately is 'closed on Thursdays' – another of my 'event missed' occasions.

As my friends in Cornwall are wont to say, "You should'a bin 'ere yesterday m'dear." Many things for people of all ages to do here. Even another boating lake where a model yacht is moving expertly in the slight wind. Of course it is being steered by remote control!

Carry on my stroll along the prom, at least half a mile long to the end. I am surrounded down below, on the beach, by very muddy terrain as the tide is well out just now! Wouldn't do to fall over the edge here!

Sit on the last bench and take out my snack lunch and Coke. 'Ting', a message on my *iPhone*.

"I see you're in Maldon," says my son on business in Tokyo. I didn't mention that I am registered on all the family's phones for 'Find Friends' where a map gives you exact details of where everyone is! I think that is why I was let loose – they can check where I am at any time!

"Yes, having a lovely time," I reply. Good job! I keep my battery charged up and *iPhone* on at all times!

I can get used to this modern age. It is quite reassuring when technology works, or rather when I know how to work it. Still more lessons to come though! Tide has turned and is coming in over the mud rapidly. Several yachts are waiting for enough water beneath their hulls, to make it to the harbour along a marked channel.

Notice the life-sized statue standing next to me: Byrhtnoth the Earldorman of Essex died aged sixty-eight having famously, I believe, single-handedly confronted the Vikings at the Battle of Maldon in AD 991. At high tide, a lovely

Thames Historic Barge called 'Hydrogen' under full sail arrives to disgorge fifty elderly visitors who have enjoyed a two-hour sail and lunch. The barge takes a good twenty minutes to come alongside, tie up, prepare the gangplank before they could usher the passengers off the barge very carefully. They were lucky to have such a lovely sunny day for it.

As the school holidays haven't started yet, there were many parents with toddlers, pushchairs and dogs enjoying the weather. It is always fun sitting and watching their antics; especially being on my own, I am invisible to them. That is until I address a toddler and he wanders over to talk to me when Mum isn't looking.

He's got his eye on my box of cheesy chips I treated myself to – no, I'd better not give him one; I expect Mum has told him not to talk to strangers. Incidentally, I have to keep the lid on my chips between mouthfuls as the pesky seagulls are gathering again. Eating outdoors is hazardous these days.

I go to explore the upper prom with another leafy park, leading to a Museum – you've guessed it – not open on Thursdays. (Event missed) Back down to Barges' moorings and watch the sailors of Hydrogen going through the lengthy ritual of spraying with fresh water all the ropes and equipment on the boat. Lots of extra work that sailors are used to, once they lower the sails, including clearing up the restaurant below decks too.

Decide to walk back up the hill to find a restaurant for supper as I am too shy to march into the busy Queen's Head on my own and find a table. I'm not used to being single yet. Tried the Jolly Sailor, there is no one in there by contrast. *Hmm I wonder why*. Up at the top – nowhere open so retrace back down again. Jolly Sailor has a few more people – in I go.

"Salmon salad and a glass of lime and soda please," and I sit near a window with the lovely Maldon view just below.

TV news: Konta lost tennis to Venus Williams. Andy Murray lost in five sets due to his bad hip. Back to my lovely *Jazz*. Home to Chelmsford with usual ritual, along lovely leafy back lanes; TomTom seems to know I like these routes! I arranged to stay here for two nights so I could study the Thames Barges at Maldon.

Note my petrol down to half now. I have three bank cards just in case: two are different bank debit cards and one is a credit card. I use the Contactless sometimes and always ask for a receipt. I keep their numbers in my 'important office folder' with all my car insurance and vital booking hotel details, all together in a convenient hessian shopping bag in the passenger well of my car. They are overseen by Dartmouth and Cuthbert. Tomorrow's clothes and box of devices are all taken in to hotel. I have to put them on charge overnight, not the clothes, the devices.

Next morning, I leave after a sumptuous breakfast with my Host at Chelmsford. Off to see nieces at Needham Market in Suffolk and stay nearby at Stowmarket. Have a lovely day with four of them, out to lunch at a local farm nursery and restaurant. Don't see them much, any more than their dad does, my brother as he now lives in Ireland. I can report their news back to him on an *iPhone* call sometime, when I can get a signal!

After a fond farewell from family I navigate a short journey to Stowmarket, where I am staying the night. The Cedars is a very smart hotel with plenty of parking for *Jazz*. Have a very tasty liver and bacon and mash for supper in their dining room. A change from going out to find somewhere. I'm not yet happy when they ask me, "Are you on your own?" or "Are you expecting someone?" When I request a table for one. Time will help, I dare say. Up two flights of stairs (mustn't use lift; I need the exercise), luckily only bringing in the necessaries from the car, amounting to three hessian bags and my handbag, I can manage OK. A pleasant room for one.

Chapter 6
Stowmarket to Sheringham

After my usual scrambled egg and mushrooms on toast and coffee, I leave the almost empty dining room, pack car and set off for Sheringham in Norfolk where I am staying two nights. My family lived near Cromer and I met my late husband at West Runton many moons ago. TT and *Jazz* take us along the back lanes with lovely scenery, so we miss Norwich etc.

It took two and a half hours to reach the YHA which is not open until 4 p.m. in Sheringham. Safe parking for *Jazz* (and hiding of TT in glove box). Go for my customary stroll to get lunch then walk along the prom. Suddenly all tourists are ignominiously swept aside as a large rubbish lorry drives along the prom and onto the lovely sandy beach.

Sometimes I think these operatives are 'jobsworths' as they laud it over us all! My home beaches of Brighton and Eastbourne are mostly pebbles. Chat to the two lifeguards Lucas and Tom on the beach. They point out the hazards, mainly rip currents, along here. They are both full time and plan to go travelling to foreign parts when they finish at the end of the summer.

The lifeboat is quite a way away from their hut so I don't manage to visit it. It is the RNLI's Open Day I discover later. Oops! Another 'event missed' on my Tour. Have pleasant time on the beach, no seagulls in attendance just then… Giant boulders have been piled up on the seashore against the sea walls. "Cost was enormous," Lucas said. "They're good for sheltering visitors from the constant wind that is always around on this North Sea area."

Oh dear panic stations – I have mislaid my *iPhone*. Walk another two miles along the seafront to look for it, eventually back to hotel. The receptionist said, "Go back to your room and I'll ring it for you." Relief! There it is, sitting on the charging bag waiting for me to deal with it! It has a black cover, so I couldn't see it! Such relief gives me a telling-off and vow to pay more attention when sorting out these aids.

Now time for supper, they only have pizza in the YHA café – so Hobson's choice it must be. They do rustle up a small glass of *Merlot* red wine for me. (I deserve it after my shock earlier.) I know my room is very cheap for two nights.

It is bunk beds – just for me on my own. When I get up there, there are four of them, two sets of two. Now how do I choose which one? The high ones won't be much good as I have to go down the ladder for a wee in the night, so I settle for a bottom one (sorry!) I can reach across to haul myself up on the opposite bottom one.

What fun! Put my clock and torch on the floor next to my slippers. The loo is down the corridor. I don't think the place is full. I haven't heard or seen more than four people about so far, so I may have it to myself. Memorise the route through the fire door and along the corridors, no creaky floorboards, so that's OK. And go to bed.

Miss breakfast as it finishes at 9 a.m. "Bye *Jazz*, have a nice day off!" Catch bus to Cromer (free with my bus pass!) for the day. Note to self: how to get Siri or whatever for free Wi-Fi on the bus? Quite sunny.

Go to my favourite Cromer pier. Very smart with ads for shows on the end of the pier, not many piers do that these days. Have a yummy breakfast on the pier, watching all the visitors arriving with all their beach paraphernalia. The tide is in, so there isn't much room among the boulders and sand at the top.

A new friend having coffee nearby explains to me, "You can book a caravan for short holidays through the Sun Reader vouchers. I suppose there will always be one or two vacancies on the vast plains of caravans that are seen all along the coast, especially here." A salutary tale that emerges on the news after I have left is a group of 'travellers' have set up on the West Runton car park suddenly. The news says, "Cromer is in shutdown as the police are called in." This is one of the major car parks for the town, so visitors will be quite upset if it is closed. No more news of it, so it must have been resolved. Lovely views along the sandstone cliffs at the seaside. Much erosion still going on here, houses tumbling down periodically.

When my family lived nearby in the 1950s, my brother and I were fascinated to creep along a narrow leafy lane near our house in a hamlet called Trimingham, five miles from Cromer to spy on a derelict, empty bungalow that was gradually sliding down the cliff slope to the beach. We weren't supposed to be there, especially as they said the beach still had land mines from the war.

Maps were no longer useful as erosion had moved the mines. One intrepid local chap could find a special way down there when there was something to investigate, such as a dead body or a consignment of grapefruit washed ashore!

Chapter 7
Cromer

My main visit to Cromer is to see the renowned lifeboat Museum along the prom and the latest lifeboat too. My family knew Henry Blogg and his family in the past and have supported the RNLI all our lives since, as we have always indulged in sailing. I mean to visit many of the two hundred and thirty-eight lifeboat stations on my Tour, but as they are all along the coast and I have to go inland a bit, I can't manage more than a few.

Also there is no one there unless there is a 'shout-out', just the Gift Shop when opened by volunteers. Get a good action photo of the RNLB Lester as it returns from an exercise. I am so near I am sprayed by the crew as they douse the boat in fresh water to get rid of all the salt!

Sit at the top on a cliff road above the pier listening to an acoustic guitar player entertaining us. He is playing all day. I hope he makes some money. I have had to buy an umbrella! Suddenly the heavens open as I am in the town centre. I rush into a shop, choose a shorty one, stand in the doorway and press the silver button to open the umbrella.

Wham! With great force, the whole thing opens in a flash. "Oops, sorry doggies." A man sheltering next to me gets a fright as do his hounds, "I'm a learner with this," I apologise. All summer visitors are equally drenched as this black cloud empties itself on us. We have to pretend we don't mind, sloshing about in flip-flops shorts and thin t-shirts. "We're British y'know." The centre of Cromer is the Church. I take a look inside. I see they still have the 'mission' on the beach for games and (in our day) prayers. We used to rush into the sea when they came round to invite us to build a giant sand castle and sing round it.

Back on bus to Sheringham, then another look around their 'tut' shops as my Mum called them. Off to supper at YHA. The worst I've had so far! Only the cider was OK. I expect the guests go over to the nearby Tesco to get their own food. At a budget hostel, they won't want to spend the money YHA is asking for meals I think.

Investigate the lounge. TV on, no one there. Youngsters are all occupied with their *iPhones*, so aren't interested in it these days. With *Netflix*, *Catch-up TV* and all other facilities that I am still not au fait with, they can choose when and where to watch items.

The shower room is immaculate, simple and does a good job for me! Use my favourite towelling robe as usual. No one else around. Have an unexpected call on *FaceTime* from my daughter and friends in Cornwall. They are walking a bit more of the Southwest Coast Path and wonder how I am. Marvellous – here I am at 10 p.m. in my comfy bunk bed talking to family in the West Country at their guesthouse. "See, I'm never alone with a phone, or *iPad* or TomTom, am I? As long as they're charged up – hey!"

Chapter 8
Skegness

"Off to Skegness please TomTom." Everything tickety – boo in my *Jazz*. My travelling wardrobe is working well, especially as I only take a few items into the room each night. Incidentally – a good tip here – if you're only staying one night, don't put anything in drawers or cupboards in the room – do as we know all our young people do – use the floor and sometimes the chair to drape everything. That way you can see all at a glance as you leave in the morning. My devices have a table, my toilet bag has a table or shelf in the en suite, my torch and clock and book on the bedside table (There isn't one in the YHA, so floor again).

A long ride from Sheringham to Skegness. My hotel is only about two hundred yards from the beach, the most convenient parking spot for *Jazz*, off the road, tucked under the dining room window of the hotel. Very prosperous-looking seaside town along the beach, together with a long pier with many seats each side.

Tide is out so all families enjoying the sand even though the sea is a long way away. All the old-fashioned amusements to be found too, including a group of very healthy donkeys giving rides along the sand. I make two new friends as I sit near the gardens. "We're Chefs from Grantham," they told me. "We go all over with our Pokémon Go, which collects points and is a fighting game. We are in competition with each other. We go all over the country.

We were in London yesterday, share the driving too." They are in their late twenties I think. Try to show me some of their moves on screen, but a bit difficult to see sideways. My Grandson informs me: "This is a successor to the Pokémon games from the 70s. It is a digital game which is mostly based in parks and open spaces. Using your *iPhone* you follow a map and instructions that point to a suspected location. The Pokémon appears on your screen so you have a success. Each one is worth a different value."

I say, "It involves a lot of walking about to find them which I suppose means getting some much-needed exercise these days, doesn't it, Lewis?"

The chaps leave to continue their game. "We've done about eight miles already."

Walk back along the lower prom towards the Seaview Pub recommended by the Lifeboat volunteer Pat. "Best food around." Maybe that, but no one around on an early Monday evening.

Have a scrumptious homemade chicken and mushroom pie, peas and new potatoes and gravy and half a pint of Stones Bitter free with meal!

Videos with old songs on the TV. Only six more people arrive for drinks when I am there. A very handy pub as my hotel is just along the road. Another very clean, smart room for a single person.

Next morning at breakfast, my hosts Roger and Alison tell me they are going to Australia at Christmastime for a big holiday. They explain how they bought this Victorian building, hadn't expected to start the bnb business, having made an annexe for their Mum (over 100 when she died), but it has worked well for them for a year so far. Their rooms and the dining room and conservatory are very smart and they are very welcoming to guests.

A standard greeting is, "The Wi-Fi details are in your room, any difficulty come down…" I'm used to this now. I know I must register with both my *iPad* and *iPhone* each time in order to have my photos available in both places. They put the codes on a tiny piece of paper, so you must enter it straightaway – presumably so you don't give it to anyone willy-nilly. Also check that *Jazz* is OK.

Chapter 9
Hull

"Now we are heading for the Humber Bridge TomTom," but first a visit to the Grimsby Heritage Centre as mentioned by my host. Very difficult to find. Just near Sainsbury's car park. Disguised as an imposing red brick warehouse, a bit disappointing as some areas are closed for a school party being escorted round.

Only one old trawler moored on the water nearby which is also closed to visitors at the moment. Make a short visit to the museum and its café and consume a very dry scone with my coffee. Then into Sainsbury's to buy a dual socket/plug for my devices. I have left mine behind in the last room. Very pleased with myself that I manage to buy the exact one I need in gold (colour), for £10. A lesson here: check plugs more carefully in rooms when leaving.

Back in *Jazz* having entered the postcode for Hull, good ole TomTom all ready to go. The Humber Bridge seemed a bit daunting, but we sail over it! A beautiful sight in the sunshine with the River Humber shining golden as we cross. It was once thought of as a white elephant, but nowadays it is taken for granted, over 120,000 vehicles cross per week. The toll is now £1.50 for cars.

Built in 1981, it is now a Grade-1 listed building. A single span bridge with each cable weighing 5,500 tonnes. (I have to note that my late Uncle's company Dorman Long is mentioned in the planning stages of the bridge.)

I have now two notches on my belt – Humber Bridge and the Dartford Tunnel. Off to the Earlsmore Hotel, Kingston-upon-Hull. Park *Jazz* outside on the road and take a tour of the nearby, local College grounds.

My hotel is in a residential street just in a very busy area on the outskirts of 'Kingston-upon-Hull'. Small parade of shops and Pearson's pub I find at the end of the road. Chat to two young ladies, aged twenty-one and twenty-two, running the pub. They advise me to use the Bus App which they download for me to go into town, as Hull is the city of Culture this year.

Another 'event missed' on my behalf; It is already 4 p.m. and I haven't registered at my hotel yet. Also bussing and wandering around a busy, strange town on my own doesn't appeal. If I had another day, I might join a tour of the city tomorrow. Next time maybe. Enormous, smart room at hotel with all facilities, double and single bed, TV, settee and tea making gear, all for me. *How can holiday companies charge single supplements of £200 for one person when such arrangements as this are available*? I wonder.

Double bay window looking out over trees and the park. Parking is at the roadside with permit supplied by the Hotel to put on dashboard of *Jazz*. Have opted out of breakfast as it finishes at 8:30 a.m. Total cost for one night is £30 via booking.com. Go back to Pearson's for double pizza night! This bargain cannot be missed. I can also have a nice glass of Merlot now I am not driving till tomorrow. See the size of the pizzas! I give one away to a group of girls nearby.

They are all dressed in their finery, except for their holey jeans with glittery off-the-shoulder tops and long flowing locks, probably on a hen night. I forget I am only one person these days and can't eat enormous pizzas, even if they are free! Back at base, set up my devices with new gold plug for the night. Give TomTom his one-hour charge on his separate plug. He'll be charged completely via *Jazz* USB tomorrow.

Chapter 10
Another Family Visit

Don't panic! Can't find my set of door keys when I go to leave. Rush upstairs with a friendly lady who comes to help me search my large room. Eventually find them in my dressing gown pocket, didn't know it had two pockets... Another lesson: Must be more careful with keys.

TT had a job getting me round Hull, not wanting to go over the Humber Bridge again! Jazz didn't say a word (nor did Dartmouth or Cuthbert). I did at least two circuits of the large roundabout before we got going towards Newton Aycliffe near Darlington to see my cousin. Stop at Wetherby Services to get some flowers, have a wee and a coffee as usual. Journey a bit more taxing than I want. Note to self: Make sure the next bookings are not more than eighty miles long. I did two and a half hours this morning. This is a leisurely Tour after all!

Very affectionate welcome by my Cousin at lunchtime. We have lots to talk about. She has to go to work for two hours this afternoon, a good time for me to book some more of my rooms further north. We have a lovely chicken Kiev supper with husband, Mike. Tonight is Quiz night at the local pub Cobblers' Hall. I have been invited to join cousin and friend in their team. With a bottle of wine to help us along, we have a fun evening, even though we don't win! Very nice night in their spare room surrounded by lots of books and a shelf devoted to all their motorbike helmets.

Next day see on Find Friends that son who was in Tokyo is just arriving at Heathrow. We take a trip to Tesco's to top up my fruit stock in the cool bag in the car: blueberries, pears, nectarines and bananas. Yet another scare as we get home – my car keys are missing. Cousin doesn't panic – we find them on the floor of the car near my seat. I had been struggling to put my waterproof on as we drove to Tesco's and they fell out of my pocket. Yet one more admonition to BE CAREFUL when putting keys away.

A mutual friend arrives for tea and I chat with her eight-year-old daughter now on holiday. She uses an *iPad* (the eight-year-old I mean). I was very interested for her to show me the games or fashion items that she puts together. No time to talk to us though! The way of the world for youngsters these days.

Have some of cousin's special tea bread with Lurpak Spreadable butter on it. Must get that at home. Trouble is it's so spreadable I'll put too much on! Cousin irons tomorrow's trews for me – She says, "you must roll your clothes. They don't get so creased that way."

When she leaves for work, I book Aberdeen for two days' ahead. Later on we go off into the picturesque Northern countryside to a renovated olde worlde pub called The Spotted Dog for supper – salmon fillet, mash, veg and tasty sauce. Treated by Cousins. So home for more chat, photo and bed.

Chapter 11
Berwick-on-Tweed – Mordington

Next morning saying farewell to cousins, on the way to Mordington near Berwick on Tweed, a tiny little picturesque hamlet that doesn't seem to figure on many maps. Stop at Seaton Burn for pancakes and coffee. Just a good distance for a break after motorway driving.

After fascinating scenery all around, by-passing Newcastle, Morpeth and Alnwick we are directed for the last five hundred yards by the local postman to our destination for the night. Sign in at the Old School House, Mordington dated 1840, parking Jazz at a convenient lay-by near the house.

I then leave for an interesting walk around the village. Such a tiny spot among green, damp very high hills. There are several bungalows with beautiful floral borders facing a green thing called 'clappers'. Mr Clapper built three houses for his spinster daughters and his estate lapsed as he had no heirs.

Now I believe they are all privately owned. The other houses were built for WWI veterans as small holdings where they were encouraged to garden and keep animals. The village is surrounded by fields and woods and should feature on calendars and postcards as it is so pretty.

No shops, just a post box. My room for the night is in an amazing museum-like house. Up a fine carpeted staircase flanked by many oil portraits of ancestors. It turns out they are all related to my host who sports a double-barrelled surname and his wife who has a double-barrelled first name. She makes lovely jams and marmalade for sale for charity, in her cavernous kitchen which I glimpse from the Library which is the breakfast room too. Books from floor to ceiling and on the floor.

An old piano in the corner and many mixed-design chairs spread about. I think they must have meetings here. My photo didn't come out as the room was too dark for my amateur attempt. In my private loo, there is an enormous photo of the Flying Scotsman train. At home, I saw the real one coming to our town earlier this year on a countrywide tour. My room sports a double, a single and two bunk beds and a washbasin.

More interesting portraits all around, at least two Persian carpets. Some heavy antique furniture well spread out in this enormous room. My tea tray was another delight (for an oldy): China cups and saucers, milk jug and teapot and silver teaspoons. Sugar and sachets all in antique china bowls too.

At the side are two A4 sheets of instructions for guests, including a list of breakfast dishes and exactly what time I would like it – 9:10 a.m. I choose. "Fill in the list and leave on the bench on the landing by 9 p.m. please."

I duly follow all instructions, especially the ones about using the ancient shower in the nearby bathroom! The view from my first floor window is equally delightful – across the narrow road and hedges to a distant hill and woods that would make a scenic painting if I were here for longer. Oh, and another note of course on the table – the pass code for the Wi-Fi.

Enjoy making my coffee, then after another stroll along a couple of fields near the house I meet Anita, a smartly dressed middle-aged lady from further South I gather from her accent, who has recently moved here with her husband. She tells me some history of the village and that the owner of my Old School House is a retired modern history lecturer. Mordington is right on the Scotland/England border.

We discuss that our family clan the warring Johnstons would have been nearby and Anita said, "I'm a Graham. We might have been fighting you!" Surely my host could give us all the details if we ask him! She gives me a tip for supper – "Go to the Meadow House pub just three miles away. It is described as the first pub in England and the last one in

Scotland." Indeed the meal is very good. Study other diners taking giant mouthfuls of food, another family all looking alike with very big aquiline noses.

Children enjoy the bouncy castle in the garden, not worried about the showers that have made the whole edifice rather wet. I enjoy this very pleasant interlude, having had to wake Jazz up for an unusual outing in the evening. I can't have my customary glass of Merlot, as I never drink alcohol when I am driving; I don't even indulge in Tiramasu for dessert either! This short journey makes a very pleasant interlude. Drive back to Old School House, luckily parking for Jazz is where I left it! Usual chores and planning for tomorrow.

Chapter 12
Kinross

After an ample breakfast in the library, chat to my hosts. Buy a jar of their marmalade for my friends at home. Have to dig out my chequebook to pay my dues, that's how I learn their special names. What a good job I elect to have a meal before I start in the morning!

This morning is distinctly wet and dreary-looking. TT takes *Jazz* and me over hills and dales and flooded tracks as a short cut to my next destination! One amusing thing – TT takes me along a very narrow farm track with numerous potholes. *Surely this is wrong; did I put an incorrect postcode in?* I ask myself. Surely I can't disbelieve TT after all we've been through?

I stop at the first field gateway we come to. *I'll turn round and restart,* I think. Great difficulty negotiating the overhanging wet hedges and dripping trees and proceed slowly down the muddy track. Suddenly, "Turn around when possible," says a familiar Australian voice in my ear! Well. "Blow me. We were going the right way after all." TomTom doesn't say that, I do! Nothing else for it – turn round when I get out of this tiny lane and retrace our steps (sorry – drive) up the muddy track again!

I remember the sign I once saw on my travels that says, "Test your brakes," as we come across a flooded farm track at the bottom of a steep hill. Good ole Jazz is up to the task as usual! Pot-holed to Ayton, then on A1 – tarmac at last – towards Edinburgh. We bypass this famous city – visit it on another occasion, when I am not so busy learning technological operations!

Realise my petrol gauge is now reading a quarter and there is no garage on this main road so far. I'm sure my *Honda Jazz* does many miles to the gallon, but still, I must be aware of such things. Eventually after about another forty miles in the picturesque, but rainy countryside, I come across a side road to Tranent which has a signpost with a petrol pump sign on it. What a relief! Oops, "No, it's just a car wash, lady," said the very Scottish-sounding man in the office on the old garage area as I stop nearby.

Don't panic, I said to myself.

"Just go down the road a wee way and you'll see the forecourt on the left," he affirms.

"Aye, I'll do that," I hear my best Scottish lilt comes out as I wave 'thank you' and get back in Jazz. Follow his directions, fill up and then go into ASDA for two coffees and teacake to recover! Change in Scottish notes now and Scottish accent prevalent everywhere.

I wasn't going to mention the diabolical weather that is dogging me wherever I am at the moment, but it is horrendous.

Luckily, the Scottish drivers automatically drop their speed to forty or so when it is bad – maybe because they can't see any more than me. My Jazz boot lid is a bonus when I'm out there sorting my wardrobe. It is a good shelter. Yet more stunning Scottish scenery, albeit shrouded in misty rain most of the time.

Jazz is just the right size for these narrow Scottish lanes. TT takes me across small, long country trails to miss a lot of traffic, popping us out suddenly on a motorway from a tiny insignificant side road. It probably saves time as I think TT's route is called 'the fastest route', though I'm not sure it is in the end. I enjoy it though as I'm not in a hurry, as I keep telling us!

We go over the Forth Bridge after a few more of my own detours – TT doesn't get fazed, just says, "At the next roundabout take the fourth exit," not telling me I've gone wrong, then "Take the first left", where I should have gone in the first place. Dartmouth and Cuthbert argue with him, but then I can't hear them.

Get to Milnathort near Kinross at about 2:30 p.m. The Thistle Hotel which is busy in the bar with sport on the TV. Good safe parking for *Jazz* round the back of hotel. Very nice room with two beds and a big bathroom and a view over the street. Crawl on floor to find socket for kettle, (manage to get up again) have coffee with fresh milk and a biscuit.

Need to calm down after a three-hour drive; remember I'm on a 'leisurely' Tour. Still no more driving today, even though I enjoy it. Rest of day off for *Jazz* too!

Off for customary walk-about after I put socks on! "Yes, it is distinctly chillier up here." Other travellers I've read don't mention their wardrobe and choice of outfits. Is it because I arrive by car and am expected to look respectable perhaps? More about my laundry later. Can't find Orwell church as mentioned on foyer leaflets, in the rain.

There is a small mall and a PO with no chance of a scenic walk, so back to room. Plenty to do there, then down to dinner in the hotel. Only about six people again in the restaurant. Thin, gaunt, tall hotel manager seems to be in sole charge of front of house, tells me in his thick Scottish accent that the menu is on the board. Have a delicious liver and bacon, mash, veggies and gravy and a glass of red wine. All right with the world now.

Ring up one or two people from my room – just because I can! Get code, press correct buttons and dispense a little of my news. It would have been that, but there is no signal in the hotel so I shall have to wait till I go to Jazz next day. In the morning we set off for Aberdeen.

Reluctantly give Loch Leven a miss as it would have been too misty to see anything. There is an interesting Loch Leven Heritage Trail which is thirteen miles long around the Loch. This would be superb in good weather, especially as the map shows several handy cafés en route. No 'event missed' on this occasion, but 'Loch missed'.

Stop at Forfar for a coffee. Tables in ASDA very near together and I spy a man trying to eat his food as a large lady leaned over close to him aiming for the adjacent table, to put her bag on the next seat, nearly sitting on his toast as she did so! He doesn't notice! Wander into the local church for a few minutes as it is Sunday and the organ is playing. When I leave the lady vicar waving hello to me, I hope it is a blessing. Only fifteen degrees up here and I am wearing my socks.

Aberdeen:

TT worked wonders from Forfar to Aberdeen directly to the Brentwood Hotel. I have chosen a hotel in the middle of Aberdeen as I am keen to see an oil town that is so far away from Sussex. Parking for Jazz is behind the residential buildings on cleared sites that make the places very snug. Jazz is OK. The main High Street is full of all the usual shops, many buses up and down, many visitors too. Walk about one and a half miles along the busy streets and down the hill to get to the beach and prom.

A vast funfair looking very permanent along the promenade, and a Chinese Circus advertised for later. (Event missed?) Quite windy, I sit in a little shelter to eat my scratch lunch and look at the angry sea. Not many sightseers today. Bit gloomy around, but never mind I'm on an adventure, aren't I?

I photographed a Dos and Don'ts notice from Aberdeen City Council on the railings!

Aberdeen City Beach: "beware: slippery rocks, surfaces and deep holes, submerged structures at high tide, do not jump, do not dive, do not surf, possible strong rip currents, beware of tides, do not kite/windsurf or sand yacht, no fishing, do not climb on structures, do not use inflatables, do not swim when red flags are present. Lifeguard service is just at weekends in July and August. Dial 999 in emergency and ask for Coastguard." Mailed it to the family and the reply was: "At least they allow picnics on the beach!"

Back up to explore more of the town, quite a hilly street is Union Street. Book in, a very nice single room with private bathroom, breakfast included in the price. I also book dinner tonight. Incidentally the seagulls here are a pest, just as they are at Brighton; don't risk buying an ice cream unless you eat it under an umbrella!

Back in room armed with Wi-Fi details, I book three more hotels in booking.com at Portsoy (near Banff), Strathpeffer which is North of Inverness and Fort Augustus, which is going South, beyond Fort William.

All quite straightforward now I have mastered the routine on my *iPad*. I am using my torch when studying the map in my room as the light is dim overhead. Portsoy is a tiny port ten minutes from Banff but I can only book one night in Banff Springs Hotel. I fancy it as I've looked down on one in Canada when we were on a walking holiday over there. Our guide kept ringing a little bell as we followed him on the mountain trail. "To tell the Bears we're coming," he said.

"The hotels are not connected," I'm told by the receptionist. Both are privately owned. This booking is my major treat for accommodation on this Tour. Before we leave for Banff, I have a passable chicken curry for dinner and did usual chores in my smart room.

Chapter 13
To Banff

Next morning a new activity: cleaning seagull poo off my car, poor Jazz. We know how poo can erode the paintwork if we leave it. Then have to go back in to wash hands thoroughly. *Why are seagulls a protected species?* I wonder.

"Do you have a laundry service?" I ask casually as I sign in at The Banff Springs Hotel?

"Yes we do, Madam. Here's a bag. Fill it and leave it outside your bedroom door and it will be returned tomorrow morning." I've always wanted to do this one day. Shall I admit how much it cost for three pairs of trousers (summer ones), four thinnish t-shirts, a micro fleece and (daringly!) two pairs of panties? Very nicely presented next day. My wardrobe considerably improved by this – £53. Palatial foyer and fantastic view from all windows of Banff beach and cliffs to walk down, near and distant Scottish hills looking mysterious in this damp, misty Scottish weather.

Good room with a shower and loo. Up two flights of stairs with my customary small hessian bags that are easy to transport. Down again collect my snack lunch from boot of car (choice of good spots in the spacious car park for *Jazz*).

Now to find the route down to the beach. Sit on a bench on a grassy bank at the top watching the angry waves below the cliffs and figure out which way to go next. Steps very steep. Find a teeny café with lots of varied things for sale; do wonder if they sell any. The lady in charge says, "We're not on the internet as it is too complicated to arrange for postage all over the world."

She has a point there. Carry on my trip down to Banff Harbour, a small haven built in sixteen hundred to aid sailors, rebuilt since then with about fifty boats moored. Along the seafront there are many cottages which must get flooded in winter storms.

Builders are actually in the middle of filling in a space between two of them; are the new owners aware of winter weather in Scotland? Some pretty grassy hills leading down to the beach from the main road, and a small car park. Not many people find this I'm sure. Manage a steep walk back up to the hotel, "The main landmark in Banff," I'd say.

Down, duly smartened up, for dinner in the restaurant overlooking the bay. Order my glass of red wine and then a long wait before my lemon sole, veg and mash in a delicious Mornay Sauce arrives. I apologise briefly to a couple at the table behind me as I move to sit facing the view, with my back to them. As they leave later they present me with a bottle of red wine with a large glassful inside. "Hope you enjoy that as you're on your own," they say.

"How considerate of you," I sit relaxing at the dinner table overlooking the beach, enjoying my unexpected treat. Through the panoramic window I watch as a tiny line of sunset appears under the dark clouds above. I bet when the weather is good the sky is beautiful at dusk from this viewpoint.

Next morning, I meet the couple Tom and Jan at breakfast and we have a chat. "We live in Oxford and decided to stay at this hotel as we are visiting two lots of elderly relatives and need this treat afterwards before driving home," they explain.

Chapter 14
Portsoy

On way to Portsoy, stop at the tiny harbour called Whitehills. Bertie the Harbour Master says the lifeboat closed in 1968. "The small Marina pays my wages!" he says. There is one fishing boat unloading its catch by winch up onto the jetty. I count four blue boxes of fish which they load into a waiting van for market. This must be a shadow of the former activity in the past here. There are no people about, just the waves pounding the black rocks and a menacing dark cloud hovering overhead.

Dartmouth, Cuthbert, TomTom and *Jazz* and I tour along a country road with rolling green hills either side. The narrow one-track road has the customary small Passing Places to keep note of. One soggy field has Highland cattle peering out from the edge of a forest near a dark woodland stream. Many fields of corn of different sorts all around, nearly ripe I'd say. I encounter the occasional large-wheeled tractor and trailer squeezing along these narrow lanes.

On the seaside of the road, I pass several small bays which serve as shelter for boats along this rocky, windy coast. The lobster pots skirting the edge of the jetty are now made with colourful ropes. I wonder idly if the lobsters see colour, or if the colours are just for the fishermen to identify their own pots?

At Portsoy down on the jetty I look in the marble shop, the Beggars Belief Café, complete with life-sized pirate standing inside the cave. The Salmon Bothy is closed on Tuesdays (event missed). The interesting concert that is advertised in each local village will be – you've guessed it – tomorrow, when I should be in Strathpeffer. (Another Event missed).

Have a delicious meat pie from the bakers. Unusually these days to find there are two homemade bakers in this little town. I choose a bench on a hill next to a sculpture of a dolphin made of wire, next to an old building wall, with a window that is just a facade on the very edge of a steep cliff to the beach. Quite a shock when you peer through the arch to see boiling surf below!

Later on exploring further, I enter the Shoe Inn, "No food, just drinks I'm afraid, the Chef went a bit loopy and so we gave him the sack." I wonder what the story is about the pub name 'The Shoe Inn'; I should've enquired when I was having my modest half pint in there. Walk up the steep hill to my hotel where there is a very convenient square in the village, which is free car parking for *Jazz*. Only one shop of any note, a charity shop that seems to be in charge in this little town.

My hotel seems very old, not open till evening and trying to drum up more custom by installing and advertising a snooker table at the end of the dining room. My slightly harassed host spends twenty minutes attempting to put my details on her computer – in the end resorting to pen and paper – "I'll get my colleague to sort it when he arrives," she says.

At least all my bookings have been OK on the Tour so far. Small bijou room with all mod cons including an ancient looking shower. Am recommended to the Station Hotel for supper – drive (with overtime for *Jazz*) out into the country and return to find it only two hundred yards on the High Street, from my hotel (that doesn't do food). Order haggis, neaps and mashed tatties in a whisky sauce. A memorable meal, followed by ice cream. Quite a few guests staying here. Internet reviews suggest it costs more than The Boyne where I am staying for the night.

Jazz home to the Market Square, fortunately my previous space still available. Usual chores of Wi-Fi, booking a future hotel and sorting clothes. Light not much good for reading; a very neat TV set on the wall, but I have a journal to write – if I don't do it every day, the adventures get blurred into each other. I must learn to do a blog for future trips as this writing makes my hands sore! More modern technology to learn! My travel clock is useful, as not all rooms have a timepiece. Book breakfast for the morning at 9 a.m.

Chapter 15
To Strathpeffer, North of Inverness

Off on a long journey round Nairn, Inverness and the Moray
Firth in the usual bad weather! I am not visiting Inverness this
time. It is the most northerly City in the UK and deserves a
special trip I feel. The large natural harbour is a gateway to
Orkney and The Shetlands. A two hundred-strong pod of
dolphins can often be seen in the bay; they are subject to a
special Scottish Law of Protection against Disturbance.

There are many historic castles around here, as well as ten
Golf Courses spread along the coast around Nairn which also
has lovely sandy beaches. Shall I mention the Whisky Trail
which I believe could be another feature of an Inverness
sojourn! One more goal would be Aviemore, the Cairngorm
National Park and a chance to go skiing in the winter.

My Husband went skiing there during a business trip years' ago. (Envy, envy…) We aren't far from both the Caledonian Canal and Loch Ness, and only two days' sailing away from Norway. The Canal gives a good starting point to the West coast of Scotland and all the other activities there. Not the least is 'bagging the Munroes'. This consists of climbing the peaks of all mountains above three thousand feet in Scotland: at the latest count there are two hundred and eighty-two, originally tabled by Sir Hugh Munroe in 1891.

Skirting Inverness and Beauly Firth, I find nowhere to stop for a break, so I pull into a private estate to take a rest and walk round the car twice (as my chiropractor advised), have a piece of fruit and a drink and then continue.

Good ole TT doing his sterling work as usual! Get to Ben Wyvis Hotel at Strathpeffer along a sweeping drive banked by Scotch Pine trees and a beautiful view from the sloping lawns of the grounds. No other cars are here just yet.

Will Jazz be surrounded by Mercedes, BMWs and other expensive vehicles, I wonder? The building has to be seen to be believed. A vast fortress of grey stone with many gables and mullioned windows, well maintained at great expense, I think. Book in to a spacious room with views over the gardens and distant woods and mountains. "Is there a tour of this interesting building?" I enquire in the foyer.

"No, there's nothing to see; the other rooms are empty apart from the ones the hotel uses," they explain.

"Have my tussle with Wi-Fi." According to reception, "It doesn't really work in the rooms; you have to come down to reception."

"Ah well, we are in the Highlands now I believe." This hotel merits a suitcase – so back to *Jazz*, sort out all items of apparel, zip up case, hang hessian bag of devices over my shoulder and make my way in a dignified fashion up the stairs, through three fire doors (I'm not so dignified now) and along to room 114. Plenty of room to 'drape' as is my custom – nothing in drawers or cupboards as it may get forgotten next morning – table for devices, bathroom shelf for toiletries. Off to village for a look round Pump Museum where we can't sample the spa water due to Health and Safety concerns. A theatre is here too (nothing on tonight – event missed) Also several imposing, mature, very high sequoia trees in the square. They are too tall to get in a photo.

Several craft shops for the visiting coaches to see. Have a tasty soup and roll in the old Station buffet which is steamingly busy. I object to the charge of £3 to look round the small Childhood Museum – this was my life in the olden days, nothing to wonder about here! This is like Tintagel in that coaches arrive and stop for an hour to give everyone a break, then off they go again. Climb up the hill to see the church. Closed and boarded up and for sale!

Walk back up hill admiring the lovely grounds and many trees making a beautiful foreground to the Highland hills all around. In hotel I find a small private 'residents' lounge and read paper, watching a few visitors arriving. Later down to lounge bar for supper, looking out again on beautiful views of spectacular Scottish hills.

Hello! A treat in store as the cinema is operating tonight (and I'm here!) showing Captain Phillips, a Tom Hank's film. Only three of us to watch it in the smart auditorium! True story of Somalian pirates attacking an American cargo ship with Tom Hanks playing the Captain.

Very dramatic film, but not very conducive to a calm walk for me up to bed, after the American Seal people and combined Navy patrols make arrests on the high seas !

A more dramatic end to the evening for me is when in my shower, which is in the bath, I can't switch the ancient taps off! Manage to duck under the very high shower rose to turn off the hot water, then the mains cold is still cascading down! Don't panic! Get out. Don towelling robe, ring reception – no reply. It is 10:50 p.m. Glasses on, go back into bathroom, have a determined two-handed try on the cold tap when kneeling down at the side of the tap-end.

I've pulled the plug out of the bath at this point. Luckily the water reluctantly stops! Phew! What is a soaking wet towelling robe between guests and staff? Next morning as I check out, I address a note to the Manager suggesting that the handyman should take a look. The room is only for a single person, so anyone less robust would find the shower difficult to manage! We're off to Fort Augustus tomorrow.

Chapter 16
Fort Augustus

Sunny morning, driving all along the side of Loch Ness, most frustrating as it is completely hidden with trees and shrubs and with no sight-seeing places to stop. Road very narrow and not suitable for all the camper vans and caravans and large cars coming the other way. What a good job *Jazz* is slim!

Make sure I keep dipped headlights on all the time and concentrate on noting 'passing places' as I motor on. Stop at Drumnadrochit for coffee. Have to, to get that name in my account! Plenty of touristy things to do and buy here, but still no view of Loch Ness. Apparently one has to walk a couple of miles along the road to Ben Leva, then still along road as farmers will not allow walkers across their land here.

The walking/cycling route does not look at all compelling from the car. I'm told the trekking around here is quite advanced. Get to Fort William, the Ben Nevis Highland Centre, as mentioned in one of the hotel brochures.

A good opportunity to have breakfast, then choose a tartan skirt as my present, and a cashmere jersey to match of course. Said 'hi' to Ben Nevis, even though he was shrouded in rainy mist. On then to Fort Augustus. A very nice surprise as it is where the Caledonian Canal meets the end of Loch Ness. My hotel is in walking distance from these.

Take the chance for a ride on a Loch Ness boat, with a guided talk. A tall, handsome chap selling teas and coffees below deck offers me a free tea! We chat and he tells me his daughter is a member of the Loch Ness lifeboat crew. They are kept very busy in the summer especially. They also help out at RTAs on the notorious A82 nearby.

Have the chance to video a Loch Ness monster as we chug along! I practise taking a 'selfie' as I lean over the edge of the boat in the pouring rain – as usual! Back on shore, sit in a pleasant restored Victorian garden and watch a group of backpackers meet and endeavour to unload themselves of their very weighty rucksacks before sitting down in the pub garden, near the canal for a rest.

This area must be only for expert ramblers, the hills are so steep and rugged. Stroll along the towpath where the boats that came through the Caledonian Canal are moored. See a group of canoeists that had been doing a charity ride to raise money to renovate the only Trestle Bridge surviving on a small tributary nearby.

Very smart room at Straivager's Lodge, Fort Augustus, with bathroom, shower and view of grounds. Plenty of space for *Jazz* near my room so I can decant necessities as and when. Remember my own towel for this hotel as it more a hostel than a hotel. Only £35 for the room. They also run a large campsite nearby.

Wi-Fi not working here. "The kids at the campsite use it all the time, near the shower block, so I don't expect you'll have a chance," the receptionist remarks. So I use my telephone to contact family tonight! Stroll back along to the tourist area. Most of the visitors have left now on their coaches.

The Caledonian Canal is famous in Scotland for having made a passageway from East coast at Inverness to the West Coast at Fort William. It was designed by Thomas Telford and finished in 1822. It was an enormous benefit to all fishermen who no longer had to brave the long, hazardous journey round the North of Scotland and the Pentland Firth to obtain herring.

When it was initially surveyed, the three narrow lochs formed a natural diagonal line across country; the total of sixty miles was only hundred feet above sea level. Above all, the average rainfall and outlets from mountain streams would be sufficient to top up the canal. The proposals to join the North Sea to the Atlantic had been suggested way back in the seventeenth century.

The government were persuaded to fund the project, not least as it would bring much-needed employment to the area and help to stop emigration. Workers would be needed to build roads and bridges to support the project. Two towns were developed at either end: Oban in the West and Cromarty in the East to take freight from all around the world. The area is well-worth a visit, not least to appreciate the history of the development and its effects.

Have a delicious Chinese chicken curry at the Lock Inn at the side of the canal. Very busy evening, a nice change after all the sparsely peopled restaurants I've seen so far. Chat to a couple from Sidmouth who have just got back from a coach trip to Skye. They flew up from Bournemouth to Edinburgh for the start. All little cafés and boutiques shut now. One cottage garden has masses of old paperback books for sale in aid of a local charity, they will soon be worth antique money, especially the old hardback Reader's Digest ones still with their paper dust jackets on!

Back to room, still no Wi-Fi. Also I don't know how to recharge my Anker portable battery charger. That is a question to ask my gurus when I next speak to them. Bit chilly here too.

Oban:

Next morning, *Jazz* and I leave for Oban along very winding, narrow roads. For a break I visit the Scottish Sealife Sanctuary just outside Oban. The sea horses are fascinating. Also watch a serious programme of recuperating seals with their separate recovery pools.

Most picturesque scenery across the moors and past a still very misty Ben Nevis. On to McCaigh's next to Claredon Hotel in Oban. A very striking old building in blue and yellow. Being greeted enthusiastically as I enter the bar, the host asks for cash for the room first and then takes me through the bar to the hotel upstairs. A spacious rather worn-out establishment.

Up to the second floor for my room. The Yale lock has signs of having been replaced lately (?) but seems efficient anyway; the door is ill-fitting. The room has black curtains, dark mauve walls and two single beds with stripey duvets and black bed heads. The bathroom is in need of TLC. But perfectly adequate for me, although the loo rocked a bit! The bed I choose is very comfy; the bedside light gives up the ghost as I switch it on! Otherwise it is perfectly serviceable. 'The room is held together with paint and cables,' I note in my journal. The best part is the lounge where Wi-Fi is available! The long room on the first floor sports several settees, a library, some gym equipment and two arty candelabras, one not working. I am able to spread out all my 'office' over the large dining table and book my next three hotels.

Such luxury as the lighting is bright and my map is legible! Having come into the hotel through the pub, I have an enormous front door key to come out of the original Claredon Hotel through the large original blue-painted door of solid oak. Yes, I do practise the key before I leave for supper! Have to leave my *Jazz* in a paying car park till 6 p.m. then free, and leave before 9:05 a.m. next day. This means early breakfast, which I duly book.

Off to explore Oban; two pretty sandy bays, although with many rusting but serviceable, fishing boats along its harbour. Several interesting shops and restaurants along the front and a large, colourful flower bed in the centre. I read a very comprehensive Guide to Oban, including Diving to See Puffins, visit the Chocolate Company, the Smokery, the Distillery when 'Monday is a popular day to come' to mention just a few! Cruise ships stop here briefly, filling up the area with visitors for a couple of hours then leaving again. The Caledonian/MacBrayne ferry leaves from here for all the islands.

I see McCaig's Tower on the hill looking down at superb views of Oban and across the sea to Mull and other islands. JS McCaigh was a banker who owned property in Oban, including I think, the Claredon Hotel where I am staying – the pub below is called 'McCaig's' – he decided to employ many out-of-work stone masons in the winter to build a memorial to his family on a superb look-out point above the town. I didn't manage to get up there as the sky was very misty and wet!

I choose a fish restaurant called EE-USK for a fresh haddock fish cake and chips and peas. There are many people in this one, making for a pleasant evening of watching, for me! Home through main door rather than the bar at my hotel, back up the most ornate two-storey staircase with once-expensive carpet, to my room. Just enough light to read a few pages and do my journal.

Chaotic breakfast as there is only one harassed waitress to serve all twelve guests at once. She runs everywhere and clatters the plates, cupboard doors and cutlery, as if she were playing percussion in a band. The food is good and hot, having been rushed from the kitchen wherever it was! I take pity on her and leave a £2 tip. The most unusual stay which colours my whole Tour! I am later told by a friendly local, "You stayed there? It used to be known as the Fishermen's Fighting pub in the old days."

Make it to the car park just in time (9:10 a.m. actually), no ticket. The notice board said, "Every fifteen minutes over the time, £1 is charged." No ticket on *Jazz*'s windscreen so quickly set TT on the dashboard and we set off for Connel.

Chapter 17
Connel

Stop off at a small harbour called Dunstaffnage Marina near Oban. A lovely natural bay with many yachts moored there. I chat to the owners of the Marina David and Julie Banks, who run charter boats. They have twelve out today, all about thirty-one feet in length. They also have a very well stocked chandlery, repair yard and workshop on site.

A small shop for all yachtsmen's needs before they head off out to sea is the other facility. Above them on the cliffs is a fascinating hotel called Wide-Mouthed Frog. It overlooks the harbour with lovely views across the hills all around. The hotel specialises in wedding weekends, having a superb backdrop for photos. Arrive at Connel, an imposing hotel on the hillside called Falls of Lora Hotel. I take just a sample of clothes and belongings up the thirteen steps at the entrance at the top of the hill. Sign in and go for walkabout leaving my trusty steed (and hidden TT) in the car park. St Oran's Church is very well cared for and very tiny.

Nearby again up the hill is the old railway station which has the occasional train to Oban. Meet a rambler who is finishing his trek and going off on a wildlife cruise to St Kilda with eleven other walkers. He's not sure if they could go over today; they have to wait for suitable weather for the ferry when they all arrive. While he waits for the train, he shows me some photos of wildlife he has taken so far.

I had heard tell of the Falls of Lora which are near. A local lady explains. "Well, they're not high falls you understand, just fairly flat waves except at low and high tide. When the loch meets the sea at these times it makes for a special current which goes down very deep. Experienced divers come here specially to experience the motion." I go off along the path at the edge of the Loch to find the viewpoint under the Connel Bridge.

As my new friend said, "Not much to see." Sitting and watching for a good half an hour, I was imagining what was happening. it wasn't high or low tide so that may be why I don't see much happening there; just a faint, curving of two opposing waves making a small white ripple under the bridge. I have to imagine the more dramatic action when the tide is high. (Event missed?)

Adjourn to the local Oyster Inn for a cream tea. They seem geared up to receiving many coach visitors when the tide is right, after they have witnessed the spectacular occurrence. I walk along the shoreline of the river and admire the gardens belonging to my hotel.

Take the chance as there is a phone signal, to ring my friend for her birthday today, from the very rocky shore of Loch Etive. So nice to keep in touch when the technology does work! My room is very well-appointed. Lots of lovely fluffy towels, so I take advantage and have a shower.

Decked out in my latest outfit, go down for dinner in the hotel. I feel one has to have fish in these parts, so order fresh haddock in a delicious cheese sauce and all trimmings. As the weather has cleared up I go for a stroll in the village. The news says, "The Oval cricket match has been rained off." I'm lucky for once to see the sun here! I'm all set to go to Paisley tomorrow.

I've chosen a full kipper for breakfast today! Such a surprise as I've forgotten the knack of filleting them! Still make a good stab at it. I notice two Chinese girls looking at my plate as they studied the menu. I get the distinct impression that the waitress is dissuading them from trying unfamiliar kippers! They spend a long time trying to eat their traditional Scottish breakfast, not being able to understand what black pudding is! Leave as usual with TT ready and *Jazz* raring to go.

As we arrive at Paisley there are great road works going on. After about three attempts we make the entrance to the Watermill Hotel. Parking near the building is allowed – a safe refuge for *Jazz*. This is certainly a spectacular place at the edge of Paisley town (aiming to be called a City soon). The river Clyde is the main feature of this area. In days of yore, it was a mecca for transport of everything to do with the main business of Coates and Hamill, which were the cotton mills.

They built all the architectural buildings around. The main warehouse opposite the Watermill is now flats, but at least the building is preserved. Chrysler was another industry here. Not far to Glasgow too. The Watermill of the hotel name used the river which is just below the dining room window. "The pieces of mill grinding wheel cogs and other artefacts from working days are preserved within the hotel including in the cellar, which floods," explained the chef.

Now a technological breakthrough for me, "The Wi-Fi is automatically loaded onto your devices," I am told.

"Why can't they all do that?" I ask reception. Going for my walkabout over the bridge of the River Cart, I notice an island of Himalayan Balsam wild flowers forming an island in the river. It does look pretty though I am aware that it is considered an invasive plant in this country and should be destroyed. Have just found a quiet garden near the Abbey to have my scratch lunch.

Chapter 18
Paisley

Not much open in Paisley today as it is Sunday. Walk up the hill past picturesque buildings which are well preserved but not much used I think.

Have found the Paisley Museum open. A feature is the wide set of steps up to the entrance. Many cabinets holding ceramics and dinosaur footprints, but not much sign of the Paisley shawls that were famous from here. "The museum is shutting for refurbishment for four years," a volunteer tells me. "It will still be shut when and if we are granted City of Culture in 2020," she explained.

There are flags attached to lampposts all along the streets anticipating the grant of this award, but I couldn't see how they could get it. Maybe they will get a sum of money to help them be successful. I find a small group of Paisley shawls upstairs in another exhibition room, together with an enormous, very dusty, wooden loom that has been left neglected without lighting at one end of the room. "The shawls are all made in China nowadays," says a guide. Following a trail of old trades on photos on the walls, boilermakers, abattoirs, car makers. Life was very busy years' ago. Now they are hoping for the tourist boom to come here in 2020. Out again to continue my walk. Paisley Abbey shut till 10 a.m. Monday.

Hurray, I can delay my departure and visit it after breakfast tomorrow. (An event not to be missed). Book breakfast. Tonight I am dining in the lounge bar, as folk are watching a very funny kart-racing contest where all the karts are handmade to look like ducks, cars, Mickey Mouse and so on. T.V is made for these visual games I think – more action and less sitting in front of the camera talking! I always want to see the band playing on the football pitch at half time – the chaps could still talk as well…

After a substantial repast, I pack up *Jazz*, hand in my keys and make for the Abbey, leaving Jazz expectantly awaiting my return. Paisley Abbey, founded in 1163 as a monastery for thirteen monks. There are most unusual stained glass windows and one modern one called 'Light and Music' depicting candles and violins in the design.

An elderly lady volunteer, with wispy hair and a thick cardy (Abbeys are cold, stone places!) who was looking after her eleven-year-old grandson shows me all the artefacts then treats me to a coffee in the crypt!

Newton Stewart:

Leave for Newton Stewart on very long motorway roads and narrow, country roads through the hills and mountains. Beautiful countryside all around.

Have found a sweet little café in the village of Straiton, called The Buck café. It is opposite a big local pub which is not open. Sarah-Jane runs the café. She has lots of handmade tea cosies, plaques, paintings and various ornaments strewn about for sale. I am very pleased to come across this haven in the hills.

Order a cheesy toast sandwich and coffee. No one else around till her boyfriend pops in. He has the day off from his dad's building firm. I wonder if they're going out for a spin later. "Yes, I do everything in the firm especially brickie," he says. I know they can earn a packet if they work fast enough! Do hope Sarah-Jane's business flourishes; she does need to tend the tired plants in the window though!

Back on the road to Newton Stewart; more of the same hilly, narrow driving, I estimate I do another twenty-eight miles of it, still very wet and misty. I love this mysterious, mountainous scenery. TT is not able to pinpoint my hotel in the next village of narrow streets. Eventually find a local who points me to the correct road. Plenty of room for Jazz in my host's car park in Newton Stewart.

Now I am installed I can go for a walk with my landlady who is just going into town. "I'll show you the short cut," she says. The river Cree runs through the middle of the High Street, next to the main shopping area. One or two pleasant spots to sit overlooking it.

The Stables Guest House is the most immaculate one I have stayed at. When I compliment my host, she remarks, "I've been doing it for thirteen years now, so I hope I've got it right." I have a lovely room with very smart duvet, decor and bathroom with lots of toiletries. Good view of the garden as I'm on the ground floor. Wi-Fi working (of course) so I have booked Windermere for two nights. Have relaxing snooze after my long country drive. Another rest for Jazz as I walk into town for sustenance in the evening.

Over Creebridge to find a hotel for supper. While looking I meet a friendly young couple also seeking food, so we walk along together. She is a primary school teacher and was an air hostess for twelve years. He manages his brother's mini grill in Glasgow. I have a job understanding their Glasgow accent! She explains that they never get their *iPhones* out when out together or in company, which I applaud. "How do you rate the food here?" I ask him.

We all enjoy our meals especially as they elect to sit near me to talk about my Tour. They have a lengthy chat with the waitress whom they know; she has long, blonde straight hair which she keeps flicking over her shoulders, making her seem very young. Much to my surprise she said, "I'm looking after my grandkids tonight." I can't believe she is already a grandmother!

"Thanks for your company this evening," I say farewell to my new friends. Home up the very steep shortcut to my Guest House, managing the tricky front door key. *If all else fails, read the instructions,* I said to myself before I went out, seeing a label on the wall by the front door.

Have a comfy shower in my smart bathroom. Usual chores, then read about the Devil's Porridge Museum I may visit tomorrow on the way to Gretna. Each hotel has a beautiful colour brochure of all the interesting things to visit in each Scottish county, "provided free by each council", I'm told. They are very useful, especially if I find something that is actually going to be open on the day that I am there!

Chapter 19
Gretna

Tasty breakfast in smart conservatory; one older couple in there too, "travelling around sight-seeing", they tell me. Host ideally needs gentle background music so we don't eavesdrop on each other. Once again narrow, beautifully scenic, hilly roads to Gretna, looking out for the Devil's Porridge Museum as I get nearer to Anan. A very smart new Museum built in 2014. After getting an impromptu talk by the Vice Chairman of the museum, "What exactly is cordite?" I ask. I follow all the instructive boards about the activities of the eleven thousand girls who worked here during the First World War.

The Ministry of Munitions took over the sleepy farming hamlets of Gretna Green and Dornock in 1915 and built HM Factory Gretna over nine miles long. Cordite was described as "a new type of munitions propellant", the board says: "Nitroglycerine and gun cotton are kneaded together from opposite sides of the factory," described by Sir Arthur Conan Doyle as 'Devil's Porridge'. It could explode at any moment as the girls swirled it around in the cauldrons called Thompson Nitrating Pans, by hand. "The mixture was extruded after several more processes, into slatted drying trays in varying diameters. Then cut into required lengths – looking like thin string or cord – and carefully aligned, wrapped and packed into boxes for despatch to the filling factory."

Two complete townships were built to house the thirty thousand munitions workers, with all modern facilities including shops, schools, churches and cinemas and social welfare consideration. Some of the girls were only fifteen years' old and left home for the first time. They were all issued with uniforms. The statue in Gretna is of one of the girls wearing the distinctive 'mob cap'. There are other displays in the Museum of World War Two and the Cold War. Well worth a visit, and with a good café too!

Off to Gretna and my next hotel The Gables. Look around the famous eloping town on the border of Scotland and England. As there was not a wedding scheduled when I arrive, I spend my strolling time peering into all the shops required for an impromptu wedding: florists, dress shops, photographers, buffet and drinks providers, also the Anvil Hall.

Not far away is a Factory Outlet Shop where everything imaginable can be bought from all the well-known stores. I expect people travel from miles around to come here by coach for the day. No tartan to be found though, it isn't fashionable in the old clan colours, but can be picked up in certain shops in designer colours with only vague memories of the originals. Have a very tasty veggie supper at the hotel. No one about. In my bathroom the notice above the cold tap says, "To get cold water, please allow the water to run for a while!"

Kippers again for breakfast. Nicely filleted ones that are easy to eat. Off to Windermere today. Have a longish drive on motorway to start, then hilly, narrow single-tracks again as I notice my petrol is getting low. Jazz ought to be able to tell me, but I must read the gauge! Good ole TT doesn't indicate where there is a petrol station – at least he would if I knew how to ask him.

Nearly at Windermere I find a very friendly garage. The owner is just munching a large sandwich for his lunch. "The loo is outside then left then right then under the awning." Relieved, I stand and have my coffee as he tells me about his driving of his motorbike to and from work. He has a young girl assistant, but "It must be a bit lonely sitting here all day waiting for the occasional customer." He seems quite resigned to the job. There are enormous potholes in the entrance, quite a hazard if you don't see them in time.

Get to Thornbank Hotel on a residential street equidistant from Windermere town and Bowness where the main boat trips are. Park Jazz just outside hotel in the street, no restrictions I believe.

Chapter 20
Windermere

In my room: many rules for guests – OK I'm obedient it seems. Must state what time and if one wants breakfast in the morning. I'm staying two nights as I thought there'd be lots to see and the chance of a boat trip and/or lunch on board to survey the scenery. Jane (host) will do a wash for me in the morning.

Read about three nice scenic, hilly walks from here, but don't think I can do them on my own. Choose the route on foot to Bowness to begin with – it's downhill and past lots of souvenir shops and restaurants. Very narrow pavements which are tricky as we are all carrying various sizes of umbrellas.

Did I mention that it is raining? Never seen so many Asian people with so many varied coloured ponchos, plastic macs and above all tiny children carrying umbrellas that catch you at the back of your knee if you're not careful! Don't fancy a boat trip in the rain, all the windows are steamed up and upstairs the seats are all sodden.

I retire into a friendly café and sit watching the visitors making the best of it outside. Walking along the harbour, I count over two hundred birds being fed by tourists – swans, Canada geese, mallard ducks, seagulls and coots. Luckily the rain washes the poo away!

Watch two more boats come in and go out again, quite full too. If you just come for the day, you have to do it! Soaking trainers, I return to 'my' café for some lunch. "You're back again," they greet me as a friend when I sit down and try and drape my mac over the chair, hiding my dripping feet under the table. Yummy baguette of rich, coronation chicken, very difficult to eat but who cares, it's comfort food today. "And another cappuccino please."

Back up the hill. Obey the sign to 'leave outdoor shoes in the tray please' at the bottom of the stairs and get my washing ready to hand over to Jane. Make a nice brew and drape things around to dry. I've seen a nice restaurant mentioned in the local brochure, just a few hundred yards from here.

Beresford Restaurant, quite spacious with a basement room for sport watching and quite a few awards for food. Trout was delicious. Back at the ranch, I managed to follow the instructions for the shower successfully (my towelling robe too) and had a relaxing evening in another comfy bedroom. Thank you, booking.com.

After a substantial breakfast I put on my waterproof gear to explore the Sheriff's Wood on the way to Windermere. A pleasant walk along a footpath at the edge of Lake Windermere, through the woods and along a stream with small waterfalls.

After about two miles I reach a clearing where a group of youngsters are having kayak trips. Not at all worried about the weather as they are all wearing wet suits these days. Leave the shore and take a long residential road up hill and past large mansions eventually reaching the tourist streets in town.

Another comfy café where I have coffee; I then come back later for lunch, having looked in all the shops and cafés along the way. More walking in the rain, total five miles by the time I get back to my hotel. "Sorry, there's a slight problem," Jane greets me as I arrive.

"You left a tissue in your trousers' pocket." Oh dear. "I've washed them all, but we need to step outside and shake everything to disperse the flecks of white before we dry them!" After profuse apologies and use of the tumble drier, I receive a smart pile of newly washed laundry.

"No charge at all," says Jane. Now going to Trattoria in Bowness for spaghetti supper and glass of wine. Then another walkabout round the bay. Sit with several Asian friends in very colourful saris and umbrellas who are sporting technical looking cameras, as the sun begins to set and the clouds clear away. The photos we get are quite good, especially the ones with silhouettes of swans in the foreground.

Back to hotel, book the Welsh stay at Tywyn.

Chapter 21
Chester

Sunshine saw TT, Jazz and me off on the tour via the M6 and round Liverpool to Chester. Very busy Friday and my first traffic jam. Forty-five minutes wait as they recover a caravan from the central reservation. Eventually get under way, stopping twice at service stations for a short break.

I arrive at the Dene Hotel, Chester, which is large but a bit run down; only one person seems to be looking after it. Still a pleasant, small room on the ground floor. TV, teeny kettle but no toiletries, so I end up using the teeny soap they supply to have my shower (had left my own in the car!). Can't be dirty after all that rain hey!

Walk into town to see the Cathedral and black and white buildings that Chester is famous for. Cathedral a bit disappointing as all the pews have gone. Henry Twells' oft quoted poem 'Time's Pace' can be seen on the side of a clock in the North-West transept of the Cathedral:

When as a child I laughed and wept,
Time crept.
When as a youth I waxed more bold,
Time strolled.
When I became a full-grown man,
Time RAN.
When older still I daily grew,
Time FLEW.
Soon I shall find, in passing on,
Time gone.

O Christ! Wilt Thou have saved me then?
Amen.

The famous clock was renovated and replaced in the clock room in 2013. They have two life-sized animals placed in the Cathedral part of an exhibition called 'The Ark'.

There is just a small part of the vast building used for worship where I sit for a few minutes. I have just been asked by the Church Verger to move as the choir are coming in to rehearse. He is rather officious – after all what harm am I doing sitting here quietly praying? I give him a 'Paddington stare' and eventually move away so he can hang his red ropes around on chrome posts and look important; though there are only a handful of visitors in the Cathedral anyway! The organist is practising too. I watch all the grown-ups taking their places, all dressed in black gowns, about twelve in all in the choir.

After half an hour they all re-group ready for a service. No children seem to be involved here. Leave for a walk along the River Dee where several narrow boats are moored, near the Lock Keepers pub. There is a band playing here later tonight. I have supper at my hotel, ordered and served by the same people I saw earlier. Only a handful of people in the restaurant as it seems to be the case these days.

Ask if I may use their hall to spread out my maps to do more bookings, as the light in my room is very dim, even with my torch I can't make out any TT routes! I take the service of the Wi-Fi for granted, now I am a seasoned traveller with adequate technological knowledge to organise things! Too dark to read in my room so sort out my devices and so to sleep! I don't have time to watch TV even though it is in every room. Too much exploring to do and techy things to learn!

Next morning I can't find the breakfast room? No one at reception. A guest shows me the way through some anonymous wooden doors and down a corridor. I smell bacon so here we are! Same waitress as last night wearing the same black, one inch false eyelashes, sexy topknot hairdo. "Hello sweetheart, sit where you like, tea or coffee darlin'?"

"Coffee please." Just four others in here. Tea arrives, never mind I'll have it for a change. The first time I've had it for ages. (I don't bother to do it in my room. I'd rather have the lie-in and wait for breakfast.)

As I've remarked before, with these stiff wrists it is a bit hazardous operating strange kettles under taps and steering soggy teabags into the bin without making a mess, so I don't risk it. I prefer coffee anyway to get my 'fix' for the morning's travels. Leave for Wales after usual ritual of setting up the various sections of Jazz. Have to stop soon as I haven't had my coffee! Didn't realise I need it!

The scenery is to die for, Welsh hills and valleys, very narrow steep-sided tracks and distant mountains in the sunshine today! Many shades of green dividing the heights of the hills – a bit of a nightmare for painters I think. Desperately looking out for a wayside café, but these days the only evidence that there used to be one, is a converted house with a large front window and empty car park.

Unpronounceable Welsh names of villages go past. What a nice surprise, I suddenly come across a sign to the Rhug Estate Farm Shop in the middle of this farmland. (It all belongs to them.) Winner of the 'Butchers on the Farm Award of the Year' among many others. I take due note of the environmental beliefs of all items stocked in the shop, the details of the local bees and so on. Must mention it to my Grandson who is now an anthropologist.

Get to Leahurst Bed and Breakfast at Tywyn, my first foray into Wales, which turns out to be two long wooden buildings near a vast campsite. Very recently built I believe. Splendid views over Cardigan Bay from here. Nearby also, is a static caravan site, very well appointed by the look of it.

All the caravans are pale green in colour and are on the seafront at this tiny town of Tywyn. A lovely spot with beautiful sandy beaches. I expect one could stay in one of these by arrangement of the Sun Reader vouchers I was told about.

Tywyn is just to the west of the more well-known Dollgellau. Lovely views of mountains including Cader Idris.

No one at home as I arrive, but there was a friendly welcome note and keys and instructions for the room. A light, spacious room with double bed, in the bathroom were new (expensive) tiles, gold taps, navy patterned wallpaper and pristine facilities. Even a towelling robe and slippers in the wardrobe. On the tea tray were glasses and a wine bottle opener, also scissors for opening coffee and tea sachets. I toy with the idea of buying a bottle to share with them when I get back, luckily I didn't as there was no one at home when I return.

Walk down to the seafront and chat to the (very young!) Warden at his hut on the prom. They are not lifeguards as they haven't had the training, just first aid and lookouts to ring coastguard if any problem. Ed is here for the summer (paid a small sum) he is at university doing a Business Masters at Nottingham. His family home is here at Tywyn. Lovely sunny day. A big mound which is man-made, in the middle of the sandy beach is to help keep the tide at bay.

Tywyn:

Ed says, "The lifeboat station at Aberdovy is a fine one, worth a visit." He says, "Visitors don't realise if they take inflatables on the sea, the wind can pull them out of range. They should really only be used in pools." Nobody out there at the moment; it is a bit windy. Watch the tide coming in round the mound. Off to town to find somewhere for supper. There is only a small café here and a small shop on the prom.

Perhaps the caravan owners cook at home and don't need anything. Fortunately I find a buzzing restaurant called The Salt Marsh Bar and café, housed in an old Victorian building with very high beams making the roof. They can't tell me its history. A lively hen party are sitting outside wearing large sombreros. I guess they're off to Spain later. Order a haloumi, avocado and olive salad and a half of Shed Head Beer which is not local as I thought, but an American recipe made in Sweden and exported here. No local beer available, as it tends to be in Sussex.

A friendly family stop to talk to me on their way out. "We've driven half way to meet some long lost friends and we're now going home." Their respective children didn't have much to say to each other, as they sat looking bored without their phones, at the table! A waitress gives me directions home from the town. I haven't set up my *iPhone* for walking instructions. Must get *au fait* with it when I get home! No phone signal anyway! Manage to book some more hotels in my room before the light fades. Generally hotel lighting has a lot to be desired!

Don't see host very much. Just there when I come down for breakfast in the conservatory. They have two shops as well as this bnb; evidence in the next-door garden shows they do building jobs too. The husband is the host here. £60 for palatial room and substantial breakfast, a good deal.

Miss out Aberdovey, TT didn't go there – my host says he was Launch Master there for many years and one of his sons is a crew of the RNLI.

Chapter 22
Lampeter

Aiming for Lampeter in the centre of Wales where my Grandson was at university. Nowhere to stop; just usual stunning hilly scenery and mountains around. Park Jazz, have a stretch and walk around her and a drink of Coke before continuing the scenic Tour in the rain. Arrive at the Black Lion Royal Hotel in the centre of Lampeter, it obviously was a prosperous market town years' ago.

The University takes up all the centre parkland area where they are welcoming newcomers to register. The museum is closed. All shops are closed – it is Sunday in Wales! Fortunately during my wanderings I come across a new café called Pedr that offers 'roast beef or chicken and all the trimmings'. How lucky is that!

Between you and me I'm not keen on my hotel menu as they only rate three in the Food Scale! Jean, the proprietor of Pedr, tells me, "I'm hoping for a five rating as I did with my other two cafés before this. I only opened on Monday and this is my first roast dinner day." I hope they do well.

Meet two A-level students working, with cups of tea at their elbows, various friends pop in to chat to them but don't stay to buy anything. Walk through the town trying to find the way to walk up the nearby hill. Disappointing as I come across a gate which says: 'Private Road' and 'keep out, no entry'. Back to sign in. As I have had a large Sunday lunch, I decide to risk the hotel for supper! 'Chef is closing the kitchen'. It's only 8 p.m.

"I see you have summer salad on the menu. Could I have that?"

"OK," says my pink-clad waitress, bustling past with an armful of plates. Quite a noisy bunch of punters in the next bar, making an unusual ambience for a change. Finish my usual glass of Merlot (not driving this evening). Up for shower and more bookings. Towels and lighting very good here! I could do a survey of facilities, couldn't I! Perhaps booking.com already does that before they put particular hotels on their list.

Have to ask the Manager to pull my rickety sash window up for me. He says, "We've not been managing this hotel for long. I have everything to renovate bit by bit, come and see the next-door room to yours. It is like a bomb site in there," he explains. I realise they have plenty to do to update everything and admire his application. They have only one waitress tonight. She does reception and wears a pink hoodie when she takes our orders. Maybe she is new management too?

Next morning, we leave for Pontypool and cross the Brecon Beacons.

Chapter 23
Pontypool

Sunny, scenic route across near Aberystwyth, lots of narrow lanes and beautiful vistas emerging, of low and high hills in many shades of green and some even now beginning to turn autumnal shades. Stop at Garwnant a Forestry Commission Centre. Big walking area among the hills with an impressive children's play area. The museum is shut. Short trails mentioned for rambling, but the start is not obvious.

In this weather one needs 'stout shoes' or even walking boots for tackling even simple terrain I think in these lovely Welsh hills. I have a coffee and try to chat to the girls behind the counter, but they are real Welsh lasses and we have a laugh together at our accents, not being able to understand each other.

Continue on to next destination and find the Little Crown Hotel tucked away above the very hilly town of Pontypool. The old Hotel used to be a stop for the Miners' Forge workers where they could have a free beer, a hundred years ago, after they finished their shifts. The loos are done up to resemble a mine. The Hairy Bikers did a film here in February this year.

My new friend Daffyd the Barman and host, related some local history and directed my walk down to the town along the cycle path that runs by the hotel. About one and a half miles very steeply walking. (And it will be the opposite coming back again.) The town a bit gloomy. It is Monday, but there are many boarded-up shops and church. Pedestrianised area with just a few larger shops open.

My room is called Tirpenttwys, after the name of a mine. It is a double with shower room. Breakfast is £10. Only six (smart) bedrooms here. Sat in my room in the sun, reading my book for a change. Plenty of light in the daytime! Have supper here. At last, I meet a fellow traveller Jean. She is three years older than me and has driven six hours all the way from Fareham in Hampshire. She had a driving assessment before she left and passed with flying colours. She and I sit and chat together and she tells me she has come for a re-union with her bridesmaids from the 1950s.

She is meeting them in the morning, when I will have left for my next port of call. No signal for ringing anyone! Jean waved me off from her bedroom window as I loaded Jazz next morning.

I must describe part of my room here. It is very spacious with two large windows. The main bedroom door measures six and a half long-biros wide and is solid wood. The same with the bathroom door, quite difficult to open.

Chapter 24
Minehead

Long journey to Minehead, over the Severn Bridge, no charge this way, an impressive sight to see as we drive along. Bypass Bristol and Weston-super-Mare as per TT. Stop at services for a break as this will be my longest drive on one day. The roads are very busy. As I arrive at Minehead, the view is amazing. The Beach Hotel is right on the corner of the promenade, flanked by lovely colourful flower tubs which are meant to dissuade you from parking here.

Opposite is the West Somerset Steam Railway with a working steam engine taking visitors to and fro for twenty miles, and on display an old green engine waiting for enough funds to restore it. It is so sunny I have to change into crop trousers and find my sun hat and sandals for the first time. Jazz is ideal for a quick change! Locate white shorter trews in suitcase, open both doors on one side of the car (it makes an ideal changing room as long as there is no one else in the car park), put on summer sandals kept in the 'shoe cupboard' (the well behind the driver's seat).

A short walk to the beach with my picnic and rug. The tide is right out so the children have to content themselves with building sand castles and damming a nearby stream. Near the seawall are banks of grasses and wild flowers, further along barricades of giant boulders to keep the sea away. They say it takes about two hours for the sea to creep in over the flat sand, silently and quickly, just as in Morecombe Bay.

A shop is selling many flavours of cider, including scrumpy (a speciality of Somerset). I am not tempted. We tried it once and thought it's horrible! Lots of tourists filling up on plastic boxes of fish and chips and ice cream. Nice to see real seaside activities are not gone forever in this technological age. Yes, it is possible to lick an ice cream and thumb one's phone at the same time! I can't do that yet.

Walk a mile around the bay to get to the harbour where twelve boats looking very ungainly, wait for the tide to float them again. Arrive at The Ship That Went Aground pub, with two shops nearby and behind it the RNLI station. Just in time to have a look round and read the list of 'shouts' on the boards. This station seems remote from the tourist part of Minehead, so they don't get noticed very much. Having said that, they are having an Open Day and Harborfest with Raft racing next weekend. (Event missed.) There are two lifeboats here, a *D* class and a *C* class. They are pushed down the ramp with a powerful tractor.

A crewman explains, "The job is quite exacting as the engines have to be synchronised – boat and tractor – so they are pushed at the correct rate not to sink on entering the water! Most other boats are pulled into the sea or gravity helps them down the ramp." They told me about a lady that was on the cliffs for seventeen hours before they found her. It was filmed for the current series of lifeboat stories. She survived but if they hadn't been quick, she would have died of hypothermia.

Both lifeboats went out to find her sheltering in a cave at the bottom of the cliffs. The bigger boat couldn't get alongside, so they waited for the smaller one to get nearer, rescue her and transfer her to the bigger one to be transported to shore very quickly. I sit on the harbour and watch the tide creeping in, the boats' mooring ropes pulling tighter as the sea rises.

On the way back I take photos of the South West Coastal Path statue in a pewter colour. It depicts a folded OS map and two hands holding it open. The inscription is very difficult to read. It marks the end of the walk around the peninsula for ramblers, a total of about six hundred and thirty miles of stunning scenery. My family intend finishing their walk next month, so will no doubt do 'selfies' with the statue. They should go to the Beach Hotel for celebrations. I shall advise them so.

Back along the harbour to my hotel. Just in time as the heavens open and all the visitors scuttle to shelter or cars or home. I have a very nice spacious room with enormous bay windows and all facilities I have become used to, including a comfy double bed! The room is called Dunkery rather than a number. They all seem to be named after local hills and beauty spots.

Due to the weather, which earlier downpour continues into the evening, I decide to stay in the restaurant at the hotel for supper. They have a dining room which includes the sight of the kitchen and the three chefs working there. I feel a bit sorry for them as there are only three of us waiting for their delicious menus. "No one else is likely to come now," they tell me at reception. "The kitchen closes at 8:30 p.m." My seared fillet of salmon is very tasty.

I repair to my room later to finish a John Francombe book I brought with me – the bedroom light here is OK! Usual chores. I must mention the doors in the hotel, they open and close fiercely whether you're inside or outside them; very difficult to handle when you have armfuls of luggage. The two keys are on a large fob so you don't take them home I presume.

I am on the second floor where there are also several fire doors to negotiate. Health and Safety are really well supported here including swing doors to the street. Next door to the hotel is the Museum with a good stock of travel books, maps of the area and souvenirs. Maureen, in charge, says, "When you go to the Lifeboat Station, will you ask them to have some signs put up near the Museum with the directions to the RNLI station, as I am always being asked where it is – tell them Maureen sent you!" I duly pass on the message, "We've just had to replace Quay Road sign as someone pinched it."

The Lifeboat Shop Manager said, "We can't afford anything else!" Ah well, I have relayed the message!

Up for breakfast in the smart restaurant. The same three chefs are on duty. The older one must be in charge I think. The middle, younger one may be the main one and then there is a youngster who seems to hang on their every word and follow instructions as they whisper them to him. As they are on show to the guests, they must feel they're under scrutiny the whole time they are cooking. It makes for a fascinating observation exercise as I wait for my usual meal of orange juice, scrambled eggs and mushrooms on toast and coffee.

Programming TT with his friend Jazz, to take us south to Tintagel, our party leaves this smart seaside. Have had a challenging start as I have had to manoeuvre around the colourful flower tubs skirting the hotel. Last night's weather continues into our morning. Going through some dense woodland, I put headlights on, but they don't help (sorry Jazz). All hills bathed in wet mist with varying shades of green and snatches of autumnal orange, we chug along till we find a one-horse garage at Holsworthy, negotiate the deep potholes on the way in and fill up with petrol gratefully, as they are few and far between these days (garages, not potholes!).

Eventually I reach a Service station for a walk-about to stretch my legs and wander in to the loo, after I engage my Find Car app to get back again. I have to remember to use my *iPhone* immediately I get out of Jazz, as it needs to orientate its compass before we leave the car. "You parked here," it says reassuringly! No good thinking I'm next to that white VW because he may have gone before I get back! I've been caught like that before! Very busy Services, at Sedgemoor near Exeter. There are many students in the main queue for Burger King which seems to be the most popular food for the day.

Tintagel:

Back at Jazz, I extricate my scratch lunch to have with my cardboard coffee. (Find Car got me here successfully.) I sit on the boot edge which shelters me (from you know what) and enjoy my food, including some special homemade tea bread given to me by my cousin a couple of days ago. Two young chaps in the next-door car give me a smile, a wave and a thumbs-up, they can see I'm on my own I think, as Dartmouth and Cuthbert sit belted up on the passenger seat! Designers of my *Honda Jazz* must be British and therefore accustomed to the rain, as the boot lid is marvellous for shelter when delving into the back.

We have a long run of nearly three hours in total, more than I plan generally. I follow an enormous coach which seems to be going exactly my route down the back lanes to Tintagel. No passengers look out as all their windows are steamed up.

My hotel is off the main track at the little village of Treknow (pronounced Tree-no), a large white mansion looking out over the fields to the coastal path and the sea. Just as I park Jazz, the sun comes out. I meet my host – Room 6 at the top of the house, in the eaves with this glorious view.

Good tea tray with several interesting packets of biscuits too! With his directions, I set off along a narrow track between the fields towards the sea. This is exactly what I had hoped to be doing more often on my Tour, but circumstances dictated otherwise – a four-letter word – rain! I am so surprised to see very steep cliffs at the end. Amazing vista of sharp columns and rocky outcrops as I look over the edge which was once a slate mine. The path goes down to Hole Bay in a few miles and Tintagel the other way. This must be a good point for geologists to study.

I follow the coastal path for a mile, sometimes going rather too near the edge for my comfort! One or two tricky slate stiles to cross where I go very carefully. "Concentrate Mother," I can hear my Daughter calling! Follow (at a distance) a man and his son walking to Tintagel going slightly inland at this place. Several isolated houses and a small church on these high hills. Then up a very steep tarmac road into Tintagel and the attendant shops, cafés and galleries on this, the Main Street. Wonder about a bus or even taxi home, I don't think I'll walk the same way I came in, over difficult stiles and narrow cliff edges.

I'm in a sweet café called 'Happy Feet' having a toasted teacake and pot of tea. The owners tell me all about their plans for this newly acquired business – they have bright yellow Pokémon faces in flags all around the café and wear similar aprons. "Life is too short to be miserable," they tell me! I'm too late to go into King Arthur's Seat Museum as it's nearly 5 p.m.

"I have been there before," I explain to my new friends who are a bit perturbed that I've missed it.

"Worth a visit," they say. Having given me details of how I may walk home along the road, "There's a part with no pavement," they advise and I set off. I find a convenient bench looking over the house and scenery to the cliffs and the sea, in the late sunshine. Cows graze contentedly well away from the edge.

Arriving home with my Cornish pasty and box of salad to eat in my room, I'm quite pleased how it has all worked out today, especially the sunshine. Even so, I study my wardrobe (back seat case No. 1) and look out a warmer shirt and some socks for tomorrow. I check out my next three bookings. The view from my room is perfect, fields full of cows with their calves, sheep dotted about and hedgerows still full of wild flowers. Nature is usually further advanced in Cornwall by up to three weeks' than home in Sussex, the vegetation I mean.

There are nine cars in the car park when I look out this morning, so this beautiful building must have a full house. In fact there are fourteen people in to breakfast, which I am pleased to see, as I have had somewhat of a solitary meal at a lot of my places. They all sound Dutch, so this must be a special trip when they visit the UK.

I only have about one and a half hours' of travelling to another cousin's house for two nights at St Agnes in Cornwall. TT is finding it difficult to get underway out of this tiny village. When I take a wrong turning, he doesn't get cross and just says, "Turn around when possible. Drop those backseat drivers off at the next servo," in his broad Australian accent!

Have a good contrast in driving again today: narrow and hilly, then M5 Motorway and on to a long hold-up on the A39.

Chapter 25

St Agnes

Even when I 'arrive at my destination' as TT says, there is a big jam along the very lane where my cousin lives at St Agnes. They are just finishing tarmacing the next door driveway; cars in both directions along this very narrow lane with dry stone walls each side are insisting on attempting to pass each other to such an extent that each one has to back into someone's drive and creep out when it is clear! Lots of beeping! I hate my horn, it sounds so pale and insignificant; not that I use it much! (Sorry Jazz!).

I make a dash for it when the tarmac lorry drives away. I execute a hairpin turn into the family's drive with some aplomb! Later when we go for a leisurely walk along to the Beacon, a vantage point in this village, we have to squeeze into the hedge every few yards to allow visitors' cars to speed past. It was never like that in the days when our family came down every year for two weeks' holiday many years ago! We could park in Peter's Field and, laden with all beach gear and picnics for the whole day, saunter down the steep hill to Chapel Porth our favourite beach. No café or lifeguard in those days, but we never came to much harm!

As my cousins and I stroll along the top of the cliffs near Wheal Coates, the chimney of the tin mine nearby, we see down below, many colourful surfboards, people swimming and to me, an innovation – a lifeguard patrolling the shore on his quad bike. He is warning unsuspecting visitors that the tide is coming in, and they mustn't risk getting cut off while exploring the rocks round the corner. The heathers and gorse make a pretty backdrop to this sunny summer scene. Back to my home for two nights and a lovely tasty homemade pie for our supper.

Plans for tomorrow are very relaxed and I am happy to have a full day at the seaside with my family that I see only rarely. Snag is they have no Wi-Fi and the phone signal is nil in their house! A holiday for both Jazz and my devices! My bedroom is full to the ceiling with books of all sorts. I shall sleep well with the distant sound of the sea.

My cousins' house is dated in the inglenook fireplace 1700, and has a circular clome oven built in. The walls are over one foot thick of stone. After a good breakfast, we walk down to the town to visit St Agnes Museum which has a surfboard exhibition this week. My cousin is a museum guide. The designs on these boards are very artistic. In my day we just had plain wooden surfboards they now call 'bodyboards' which is not a very glamorous title.

I don't know if anyone actually still uses them. Off down the steep hill through the town and down Stippy-Stappy to the harbour which looks very smart nowadays. The Beach Café still sells crab salad – half-a-crown each in days of yore – there is another garden doing teas and a large building donated to the lifeguards and opened by the Duke of Kent in 2014. This beach is called Trevaunance Cove.

The lifeboat is a *D* Class one, positioned near the slipway. The car park has been slightly enlarged and the rocky path up over the cliffs has a few more steps built into it – I am happy to say. It is a pleasant visit for me to old haunts that are well maintained and improved these days. Watch lots of surfers and a group of kayakers in their bright orange boats. We go up the rocky path to Bawden Rock and turn inland to walk home in the sunshine.

After a cup of tea and a chatty afternoon, we prepare to go to a nearby pub The Victory Inn, for supper together. I enjoy having company at my table; usually it has been talking to the bar person or the waiter when I'm dining alone, although I have secret fun observing my fellow guests in various restaurants I go to in the evenings.

Home to see some of the Athletics on TV and then show cousins some of my Tour photos, including one or two successful short videos and selfies I took! My technical expertise is growing, albeit very slowly! How I deal with them when I get home is another matter. No Wi-Fi here and barely any phone signal, so I am excused the trauma of pretending I know what I am talking about! I must find out about 'roaming' when I get home!

Chapter 26
Paignton

Leaving St Agnes after a very pleasant two days, TT, Dartmouth, Cuthbert and I are on the road again with our friend Jazz. A long, uncertain drive towards Bodmin with a traffic jam on the infamous A30. A small disaster, *can you have 'small' disasters I wonder?* when TT fell off his perch on the dashboard. The sun has come out so I can't see his screen and he seems to have forgotten where we are heading.

Anyway I follow the signs to Paignton, my next venue and park near a town garden square. Put £1 in the meter and hope I can sort TT and my lunch out in that time. As I am relying on my most efficient sat nav for the whole of my Tour, I haven't printed the directions to the hotels as he takes me right to the door. Oh dear. I try the nearest shop, "We have Wi-Fi but don't know the code to tell you."

"We've never heard of the Torbay Court Hotel either, sorry." Oh dear, is this the breakdown of communications I've been dreading on the way? A town where I get lost in spite of TT, a hotel which has no record of my reservation and a town so full of Parliamentary Party bookings there is no room for me? The latter did happen once many years ago.

Don't panic! I decide to go to the library which is, I gather about half a mile away. Go and put another £1 in the meter to keep Jazz and the Meter Man happy; after eating my lunch in the sweet little park, I set off. I see a group of people chatting nearby, so as they disperse I ask the gentleman wearing a polo shirt with 'volunteer' on the label, "Have you heard of the Torbay Court Hotel please?"

He and his wife think hard and reply, "Yes, it's along the front to the left… I'll do you a map, shall I?"

He could see my perplexed face. "Yes, that would be fine, thanks," I say.

"It is just behind the Palace Hotel. You can't miss it." Back at the car, with my tiny sketch on the seat, I ignore TT who is upside down in the glove box now, in disgrace. We find the hotel, driving past umpteen amusement arcades and bouncy castles near the pier on the way.

Success! Find a good parking space behind my hotel, luckily we are early as there is an enormous coach already taking up several spaces; I must make sure Jazz will be safe for twenty-four hours, and go to sign in. A very good room with all usual mod cons. Have a snooze first, then a cuppa, change my shoes and drape my belongings around. Time for a walk-about as usual. Not far to the promenade at Paignton and the pier is also near. Did I mention it is sunny here!

Go along the pier and buy myself a solitary donut for 80p. Has anyone tried this party trick of trying to eat a donut without licking your lips? Not easy, but less messy than an ice cream when one has stiff fingers!

Today is Harbour Festival – I arrive as they are packing up the stalls (event missed). The Beer Tent is busy and geared up for the evening. The Folk Group playing sound quite lively, I dawdle around looking at the sea along the harbour, enjoying the music. I am not brave enough to go in and order myself a pint, though I would like to. I stroll back to a nice garden overlooking the boats in the harbour and content myself with soaking up the last rays of the evening sun.

Down to dinner at the hotel. There is a coach party staying here and a comedian due in the auditorium at 9 p.m. There are no people about. Everyone stays in their room I think after their busy day sight-seeing. Only fourteen of the hundred guests appear to watch the show. I am sitting in an adjoining room finishing my mushroom risotto and glass of Merlot, so I can hear his routine. I feel rather sorry for him. It appears he relies on audience participation… I am not tempted to join in. Up in my pleasant room I have a shower and do usual chores.

TT forgiven is working OK. After I charge him up and press a few buttons, more by luck than judgement, he deigns to set our course for tomorrow.

I see the coach party finishing their breakfast, in the same room that had the rows of chairs for the show last night. It has been transformed to tables with cornflakes and rolling toasting machine which hums quietly to itself now no one is using it!

Chapter 27
Lyme Regis

Jazz sets us off from Paignton. TT is quite happy again, being securely fixed to the dashboard and already giving me starting instructions, "At the end of the road, turn left."

"Thank goodness we're a team now TT. Let's motor!" says I (or is it 'me'!). Off to Lyme Regis and there isn't much traffic about for a Sunday morning.

Get directly to friends' house out in the wilds ten miles north of Lyme Regis. Haven't ever done the trip on my own before. Remember to think about petrol; so duly fill up on the way to Hawkchurch.

Lyme Regis. Poignant reunion as our friends have been so for nearly fifty years. It is strange for me to be here alone since my husband died last year. They have an acre of beautiful garden, so I am very happy to be taken on a conducted tour of their latest projects. I don't claim to remember the names, either Latin or colloquial, of the lovely flowers. I must admire and photograph their bird feeders though. A cunning post made of two pieces of guttering stuck together with a pole inside, that the squirrels cannot climb, with two wide arms that hold the food away from said post. Must see if I can try to make one, as I am pestered with the cunning curly tailed rats (!) in my garden!

Now we try some technological applications – I'm not really surprised that we aren't successful here. No signal for the phone and only intermittent service for the Wi-Fi I'm told! In fact I have to use their landline to contact some other cousins in Worthing for my subsequent visit to them! We have lots to catch up-to-date with, so it is really a bonus that the internet is not working here!

A tasty homemade fish pie for supper and Prosecco in teeny, special glasses – "We can have at least three as they're so small," announces my host.

"We're not driving tonight either," I say.

They introduce me to a very funny DVD called 'The Booze Cruise' later. Much laughter all round.

No need to look at my devices as no one can get me here! Must check the battery charge figures though.

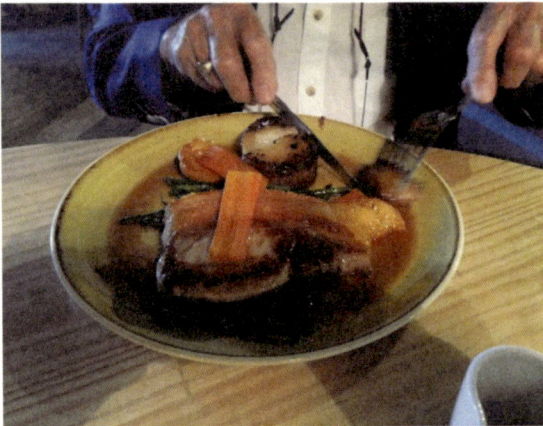

Lovely friend has put all my laundry in the wash for me. Dried and ironed too! I could go for lots more days on my Tour now! "Where would you like to go today?" they ask. In the past when we were four, it would be a long country walk and a pub lunch, but our days of hiking up Golden Cap and down again before lunch are now no more. My choice today is a trip to Lyme Bay along their narrow winded lanes in their car, the harbour and Lifeboat Station.

The friends don't bat an eyelid as they agree – usually if you live at the seaside, the last thing you want to do is go there in the middle of August! We park at the top of the steep hill overlooking the harbour. The Cobb is famous for the filming of The French Lieutenant's Woman.

The sand in the bay is all imported but looks really natural, surrounding the tiny harbour filled with various pleasure and fishing boats. The harbour has these characteristic vertical ladders fixed against the wall at intervals for bringing up the fishing baskets and pots. Fishermen have a difficult time at sea anyway, but faced with this climb at the end of a hard day must be tricky for them. I must 'think on' when I'm worried about the high cost of my favourite 'dressed crab or fresh haddock' when I am at home!

I spend time in the RNLI lifeboat Gift Shop, hearing all about the Volunteer's sailing history and life at Bradwell near the nuclear power station, before returning here to Lyme Regis. The shop is very busy and the lifeboat is well documented around the walls of the station. The lifeboat is always ready to go at a moment's notice with the crew taking their 'pagers' with them wherever they are. "I even stop in the middle of frying," says one member who owns a fish and chip shop nearby! I expect his colleagues are used to it!

My friend knows a particular homemade pie shop up the hill, so we get three yummy pies and a drink each, walk along the prom and find a quieter place to sit and eat our lunch. "Kayak hire for £10 an hour, beach hut hire in July and August £110 a week." A special note about the smaller beach being 'dog-friendly' as they're not allowed on the main one in summer.

We continue walking along the new promenade, built about four years ago which means we can get further along the seafront towards Charmouth without going down onto the sand. This area is the Jurassic Coast where people come fossil hunting. It is a bit hazardous as there are frequent cliff-falls especially when there has been torrential rain. Back up high path through pretty gardens, to our car, looking down onto the Cobb and beach in the summer sun. I'm being treated to dinner this evening at the Tytherley Arms Hotel, a lovely olde worlde pub out in the country.

Chapter 28
Worthing

Before I leave Lyme Regis, my Friend asks, "Would you like me to check your tyres and windscreen washer?"

"That would be good." He finds Jazz needs some more air in each tyre, the washer is a little short of liquid and the rest is fine.

"Plenty of petrol, so. I'm ready to go."

With fond farewells I follow TT's voice. "Turn right at the end of the drive."

"He's taking you the right way," call out my waving friends as I set off for Worthing.

Stop at a small Services for coffee briefly. Prop it up in the boot to finish later. A lovely smell wafts over to me as I drive along. "Oops," I call to Dartmouth, "I think the cup has just tipped over and coffee will be everywhere!"

At my next stop, I collect several spare tissues, ready to attack the spillage. Not as bad as I'd thought. Only a little on the empty bit of the shelf in the boot. It missed my precious towelling robe bag and new RNLI picnic bag. The exercise was just enough to give my muscles a short work-over as I walk to the furthest rubbish bin in the Services car park to dispose of the wipes. (My chiropractor would approve – the walking, not the wipes!) Back on the busy motorway, then the A27 to my cousins' flat, arriving at exactly 1 p.m. They live right next to the sea, so have a beautiful view across the Channel. After coffee and a chat Cousin and I stroll along to the Beach café for lunch. Not too full, even though it is still school holidays.

After a tasty cheese-toasty and glass of lemonade, we walk along the beach in the sunshine and sit on Cousin's favourite bench studying the waves, like you do. We also watch three elderly ladies coming down for a dip in the sea. They just had cossies and towels and flip-flops, so they must live nearby. One had a foam tube to help in the water, she wasn't as confident as the others. *How brave of them I wonder if they come every day.*

Cousin's fascinating flat is full of antiques that are always a delight to look at. They were, before retirement, in the Antiques business, so I expect they can't bear to part with their favourite items! We go through some family albums – "Don't we all look young – we all had hair as well." Cousin's husband remarks! I then show them one or two of mine taken on the Tour. (Not the whole six hundred that seem to be in the photo section of my *iPhone*). After a cuppa and an exchange of email addresses I depart for my last hotel at Lancing. What a happy interlude!

Chapter 29
Lancing

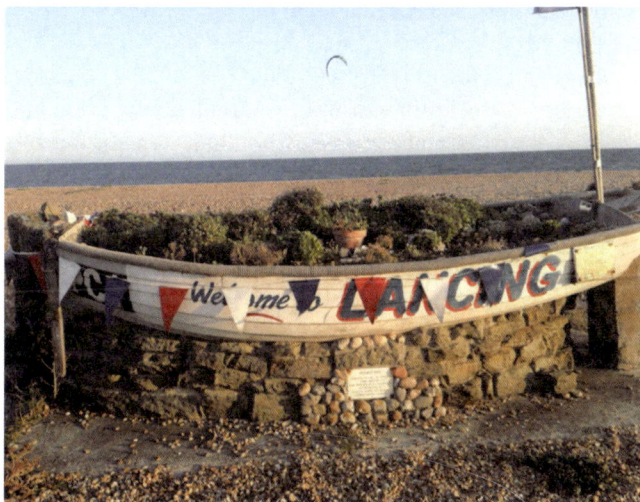

Find The New Sussex Hotel just twenty minutes along the coast at Lancing. My room called 'family de luxe' has the biggest bed I've ever seen – I think it's called queen-size, with the usual myriad of cushions and pillows. *Where do you put them so you don't trip over them in the night, on the way to the loo*, I wonder? There is a double-sized bay window looking over the prom and the sea, a useful table and chairs in the window. The tea tray is ample too. The shower room is smart and welcoming. This is an ideal finish to my Tour as home is only half-an-hour away from here. Have to have my walkabout before dinner in the hotel. The gym is closed, so is the café on the prom. There is a pretty grassy area between the hotel and the sea, cycle routes with stands for the bikes. *A*

serious exercise area here, methinks! Study the pavement so you keep off the cyclists' trail, if you remember! "Oy! Watch out you're on my path."

"Sorry," I say as I jump to one side. Not a very peaceful way of strolling along the prom. Quite a few seaborne hang-gliders sailing – or is that flying – expertly along, with their colourful sail which can suddenly disappear as they fall into the sea.

Back to the hotel for a delicious homemade chicken Kiev and all the trimmings. Only one other person partaking of food this evening. The Chef actually came out to see me. "Did you enjoy the Kiev?"

"Yes it was nice, with its crusty covering."

"I made that myself this morning," he replied.

They are renovating this hotel I gather. The dining room has wide, white-painted wooden floorboards, large windows looking out to the garden and several large pieces of furniture which must house all the dining room items. The bar is adjacent, so the atmosphere is friendly, even though the dining room is empty except for me!

Up to room to do some last statistics. I make it about twenty-five hundred miles' journey over thirty-six days. Well done, Jazz! Lots of anecdotes and amusing people to remember along the way and, fortunately, no disasters to relate.

Messages from home – Grandson has done my garden and "Do you want any milk and bread getting in Grandma?" They can see from Find Friends where I am, so suspect that I am on the home straight now. Wi-Fi works here, so does the *iPhone*.

After TT fell off dashboard at Paignton my Friend at Lyme Regis inspected it for me, "Just needs its pad cleaning with solvent, a firm twist on the base, and there you are." So TT is now good to go for the last leg.

Chapter 30
Lancing to East Grinstead (Home)

Having spread myself out luxuriously in my spacious room for the night, I now have to gather everything up, bags of clothes, office notes and towelling robe. All ready to leave for home, after a lone breakfast. Note to self: Never sit with your back to other guests (when there are some), so change the spot the waiter gestures to face the only other diner (who is burping contentedly over his 'full English'). Jazz is filled, thorough last search of room, including all devices and cables collected and we're off.

I haven't lost anything except that first night when I left my double socket plug at the hotel. My son remarks, "I expect they've got a selection you could choose from in any of the hotels, if you've lost yours." I felt pleased with myself that I knew how to buy a new one at my next stop (Sainsbury's actually!). All intact at the end! A sunny day to drive in.

Small snag to report – must have pressed the volume button on TT as I went to Jazz on this last morning. His voice is so low I can't have the radio on as we drive along in case I miss him! (Don't want to sit around trying different things at this stage.) Another lesson when I get home, "By the way, Grandson, where is the volume control on TT please?"

Anyway, I know the way from here: My constant companion on this adventure has now lost his voice which will no doubt be fully restored when we get home! Ironically, as I near home, the inevitable traffic jam catches me short, about two miles away. Turn around and pursue the long route to miss it.

Then two hundred yards from destination (as TT would say). "Road up – Diversion." Luckily, it's my town, so I find the way, but for strangers, the 'diversion' is not followed up properly, so I wonder where they go! The last test of my *Honda Jazz* driving skills: "You have reached your destination. Windows up, put on your sunnies and don't let the seagulls steal your chips."

THE END